Opportunity Analysis:
Business Ideas, Identification and Evaluation
2nd Edition

by Mary Beth Izard

ACHĒVE

consulting inc.

www.consultACH.com
913-522-6184

Published by Achēve Consulting Inc.
913-522-6184
www.consultACH.com

Printed in the United States of America

This book is written as a guide to the entrepreneurial planning process. In this book, the author and publisher are not engaged in rendering legal, financial, accounting, or other professional advice and services. This book is sold with the understanding that the reader will not interpret the information included as such. It is recommended that the reader check with the appropriate experts, such as a qualified attorney or accountant, for specific answers or for professional services.

Snapshots of Entrepreneurs and entrepreneurial examples are based on the hundreds, if not thousands, of entrepreneurs the author has met over the years. The names of some of these entrepreneurs have been changed to provide anonymity.

Throughout the book, Web sites are identified. This is not to be construed as endorsements of the specific Web sites or organizations.

To Order

Opportunity Analysis: Business Ideas, Identification and Evaluation , ISBN 978-0-9728748-4-7
  (includes Student Workbook activities)
Student Workbook activities in loose-leaf, shrink-wrapped format, ISBN 978-0-9728748-5-4

Fulfillment Plus
P.O.B. 12444
North Kansas City, MO 64116
816-221-4700
e-mail: workbook@fulfillment-kc.com

or

Achēve Consulting Inc.
913-522-6184
E-mail: mbizard@consultACH.com
 www.consultAch.com

This book is written for those who:

- Are exploring the idea of starting a business.
- Want to start a business but have no idea of what type of business to start.
- Have a vague idea for a business or are thinking about several possibilities.
- Have an idea for a business but are unsure about it.
- Have a specific idea but want to investigate its viability.

Opportunity Analysis:
Business Ideas, Identification and Evaluation

This guide takes the reader through a 4-step process to identify and evaluate business ideas, culminating with an idea that fits the reader's skills, talents, and goals and the marketplace.

Readers will:
- Learn from other entrepreneurs and how they identified their business ideas and launched their businesses.
- Identify ideas that fit their strengths and goals.
- Identify market opportunities that result from trends and unmet customer needs.
- Conduct basic market research to screen ideas and gauge potential consumer response.
- Plan next steps for starting their businesses.

About the Author

Mary Beth Izard is a professor emeritus, entrepreneur, author, and consultant in the field of entrepreneurship. She has worked with hundreds of aspiring entrepreneurs over the years and written entrepreneurship curriculum as a member of the curriculum development team for the Ewing Marion Kauffman Foundation's *FastTrac®* programs and the college course *Planning the Entrepreneurial Venture.* Mary Beth developed and launched the nationally recognized Entrepreneurship Program at Johnson County Community College and was a member of the founding board of NACCE, National Association for Community College Entrepreneurship. She is the author of *BoomerPreneurs, How Baby Boomers Can Start Their Own Business, Make Money and Enjoy Life* and *Finding the Shoe That Fits.* Her entrepreneurial experience includes real estate, light manufacturing, and consulting.

Why this book was written

After years of teaching college students and adults the business planning process and how to write a business plan, it became apparent that individuals could save much time and energy by expending more effort on the front end—identifying and evaluating potential business ideas prior to writing a business plan or starting a business. Many times the ideas individuals have do not fit their goals and talents. The market viability of their idea is often an afterthought.

When these facts become apparent to individuals as they write plans, often they lose interest and abandon the process. How much more meaningful would it be if individuals BEGAN the planning process with a well thought out idea? The purpose of this book is to fill that gap and assist individuals in identifying ideas that fit them and the marketplace *prior* to writing a business plan and/or starting a business.

Acknowledgments

I am most appreciative of my peers and colleagues who have supported my entrepreneurial interest over the years. A special thanks goes to Donna Duffey for her invaluable contributions and feedback on the *Opportunity Analysis* textbook and *Student Workbook* activities and her help in communicating its availability of *Opportunity Analysis* to others in the field. Many friends and colleagues have contributed their ideas over the years, including Beverly White, Kathy Knadlman, and Melody Kamerer, professor at Butler County Community College. Thank you to Greg Gildersleeve for his fine work editing this book. And of course, thank you and love to my biggest supporters, Brooke and Blair, my daughters, and my husband, Jack Kelsh. I would also like to thank the hundreds of present and future entrepreneurs I have met over the years who have made my work both exciting and rewarding.

Table of Contents

Step 0

Opportunity Analysis Foundations

Step 0 Objective

To build the foundation for identifying and evaluating business ideas through

- Determining the point at which you are starting this course.
- Examining personal macro issues, such as work-life preferences and goals.
- Gaining an overview of the idea exploration and evaluation process.
- Previewing the layout and content of the *Opportunity Analysis* book.

Chapter 1

Getting Started

How many times have you talked with someone who said, "I'd love to start my own business. I just don't know what type of business to start." Perhaps you have said this yourself. There are hundreds of books on the shelves of bookstores and on the Internet on how to start a business and write a business plan. Without a business idea, however, there is no business to start or plan to write.

In order to join the 6,780,000 individuals who create new businesses annually in the United States (*Kauffman Index of Entrepreneurial Activity 1996-2010, March 2011*), you need an idea for a business—one that fits you and the marketplace and will lead you to accomplish your personal, professional, and financial goals.

Opportunity Analysis:
Business Ideas – Identification
and Evaluation

Goal: Finding the Key to Your
Entrepreneurial Future

Identify a business idea that fits your talents
and skills, is compatible with your financial
and personal goals, and has market viability.

1/7/2013   Copyright Achéve Consulting Inc   1

In this book, you will use a step-by-step approach to discovering a business idea that is right for you and the marketplace. You will follow the path used by other successful entrepreneurs to identify their business ideas.

Even though many of you may think to yourself, "I already have a business idea," working through the four steps and activities included in this book will help ensure that the idea you have is right for both you and the marketplace.

Having an open mind as you approach the coursework will result in one or more of the following:

- Clarifying the business idea you have.
- Generating a totally new idea.
- Refining the idea with which you started to be more in tune with your strengths and marketplace needs and trends.
- Concluding that the idea you have is either not feasible or desirable.
- Developing a strategic approach to opportunity recognition that can be used over and over again as you search for business ideas or ways to keep your business viable once it is open.

FOUR STEPS TO SUCCESS

The path to finding the key to your future, a business idea that is right for **YOU**, begins with **YOU** and is based on a two-stage process—idea identification and idea evaluation.

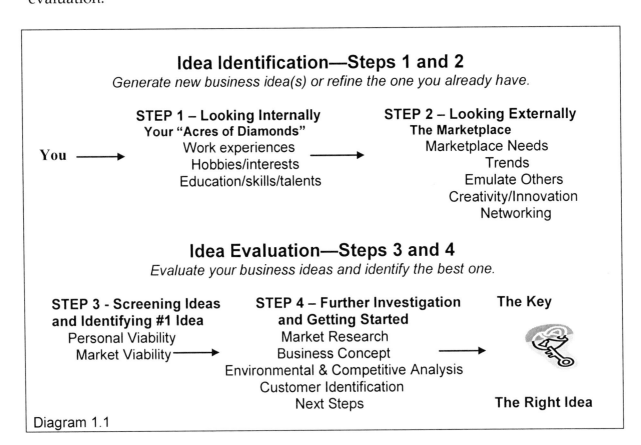

Idea Identification—Steps 1 and 2
Generate new business idea(s) or refine the one you already have.

STEP 1 – Looking Internally
Your "Acres of Diamonds"
Work experiences
Hobbies/interests
Education/skills/talents

You →

→

STEP 2 – Looking Externally
The Marketplace
Marketplace Needs
Trends
Emulate Others
Creativity/Innovation
Networking

Idea Evaluation—Steps 3 and 4
Evaluate your business ideas and identify the best one.

STEP 3 - Screening Ideas
and Identifying #1 Idea
Personal Viability
Market Viability →

STEP 4 – Further Investigation
and Getting Started
Market Research
Business Concept
Environmental & Competitive Analysis
Customer Identification
Next Steps

The Key

→

The Right Idea

Diagram 1.1

BOOK ORGANIZATION

This book is designed to guide you in a sequential process in which you generate business ideas and evaluate them for their fit with your personal skills and goals and the marketplace. This process culminates in ascertaining the idea you wish to pursue and conducting research to obtain market feedback and refine your business concept. To accomplish these goals, *Opportunity Analysis* is organized by "steps," with multiple "chapters" in each step.

Step 0, Opportunity Analysis Foundations, includes Chapters 1 and 2, and lays the foundation for the course and four-step process described in Diagram 0.1.

Step 1, Looking Internally, Your "Acres of Diamonds, includes Chapters 3-5 and guides you through the process of identifying potential business ideas based on your work experience, strengths, talents, and goals for the future. Step 1 is the piece missing from many books on entrepreneurship.

Step 2, Looking Externally, The Marketplace, includes chapters 6-10 and guides you through the exploration of marketplace needs, wants, and trends to identify potential ideas for businesses. Examining the marketplace provides a reality check for those who already have a business idea in mind or can be a productive starting point for those who don't.

Step 3, Screening Ideas and Identifying #1 Idea, includes Chapters 11-13 and directs you to evaluate business ideas based on their ability to capitalize on your strengths and marketplace needs. The research you conduct in Step 3 helps you with the evaluation process.

Step 4, Further Investigation and Getting Started, includes Chapters 14-17. In Step 4 you conduct additional research to refine your business idea and identify important next steps in the planning process.

Through the four-step process followed, you move from the idea stage to the business concept stage. A business concept includes not only a business idea but clarity regarding who the targeted customers are and how they can be reached.

After you finish this course, the next logical steps would be to continue your assessment of the viability of your business idea through research and the preparation of a Business Plan.

Activities

Throughout the textbook, references are made to activities that are included in the *Student Workbook*, a required companion piece to the *Opportunity Analysis* text. These hands-on activities are the backbone of the 4-step process followed in *Opportunity Analysis* and enable you to accomplish the objectives of the course by applying the concepts to your own personal situation. As with most worthwhile endeavors in life, the more effort and time you put into completing these activities, the more you will get out of the book and course.

Entrepreneurship Examples and Stories

The *Opportunity Analysis* book includes "Entrepreneurial Clips" and "Snapshots of Entrepreneurs" as well as a more in-depth "Featured Entrepreneur" at the end of Steps 1-4.

Early in the development of this book, plans were to include the stories of entrepreneurial superstars like those frequently highlighted in the media. As preparation of *Opportunity Analysis* progressed, it became apparent that the reader would benefit from and relate more readily to examples of more typical entrepreneurs. Entrepreneurial stories selected for inclusion in this book are designed to communicate to readers that having your own business is an achievable goal, not an unrealistic dream. Some of the entrepreneurs highlighted may indeed end up being superstars, but, for the most part, they resemble the entrepreneurs who operate businesses in your community.

> *"There are only two kinds of businesses,*
> *small businesses and formerly small businesses."*
> M. B. Izard

Data and Tips

Research data and practical tips are featured throughout the book in textboxes or comments in *Insight or Common Sense.* A word of caution: As with any decisions you make regarding your business, **perform your own research and consult with the appropriate experts** prior to acting upon any information or recommendations from entrepreneurs, experts, and this book's author.

Student Workbook

Throughout the book, the *Student Workbook* is referenced as the location of the activities you are directed to complete to accomplish the objectives of this course. *Student Workbook* activities are included in the *back* of each chapter in which they are referenced. If you will be submitting a number of these activities to your professor, you may be instructed to purchase the separate loose-leaf, shrink-wrapped *Student Workbook* to facilitate assignment submission. The packaging of student activities separately in a loose-leaf format was done in response to request from professors teaching the course. These loose-leaf pages are to be inserted into a three-ring notebook of the student's choice.

That's a brief look at the path you will follow in the upcoming pages of this book. Let's get started now by looking at the planning progression your entrepreneurial journey will take.

THE STRATEGIC PLANNING PROCESS

The strategic planning process is shown here. This book focuses on the Opportunity Analysis and Business Concept steps, which law the foundation for the entire process, yet are often skimmed over or totally overlooked.

Before you go further, now is a good time to determine the point at which you are now by completing Activity 0.1, Pre-Survey, in the *Student Workbook* pages at the back of this chapter or in the separate *Student Workbook* loose-leaf packet. This is the first of many activities you will be directed to complete as you progress through the book.

These activities guide you through the work needed to identify and evaluate business ideas.

STUDENT WORKBOOK

Go to Activity 0.1, Pre-Survey, in Student Workbook pages (included as end of the chapter or in the separate loose-leaf Student Workbook packet [as instructed by professor]) and determine where you are in the entrepreneurial strategic planning process. At the end of this book, you will complete a post survey to quantify the progress you have made.

0.1 activity
pre-survey

Directions. Answer the following questions.

1. Do you have an idea for a business about which you are excited and confident? Place "x" in the appropriate text box below.

Yes ☐   No ☐

If "yes"

What is your business idea? Briefly describe it here.

How confident are you that your idea is the right one for you and the marketplace? To answer this question, choose a number that reflects your level of confidence from the continuum below.

Write it here. ☐

Not confident   *Very confident*
0 ....1...........2............3...........4......... 5

If "no"

What have been the challenges that have kept you from identifying an idea for a business?

2. What examples do you have of when you acted entrepreneurially in your youth or childhood (i.e. Kool-Aid stand, baby sitting, lawn mowing)?

3. Why are you considering starting your own business at this time?

Chapter 2
Entrepreneurial Principles

Before you embark upon the four-step idea exploration and evaluation process described in this book, you will first want a clear understanding of what entrepreneurship is and how to succeed as an entrepreneur. The concepts discussed in this chapter lay the foundation for this understanding.

WHAT IS AN ENTREPRENEUR?

The term "entrepreneur" is used to describe a person who identifies a business opportunity, gathers the resources, and assumes the financial, emotional, and personal risks of launching and growing a business.

Having an idea for a business is just the initial step to becoming an entrepreneur. Some individuals have a business idea in mind for months, years, or forever. They may not possess the needed entrepreneurial characteristics, or, perhaps, they have not experienced the precipitating events which often trigger action (i.e., being downsized from a job, difficulty finding a job, retirement, financial distress, desire to be one's own boss).

Theories on what drives an entrepreneur have been around for decades. Renowned economist Joseph Shumpeter was one of the first to venture into the unchartered waters of the entrepreneurial psyche in his book, *The Theory of Economic Development.* Shumpeter said entrepreneurs feel "the will to conquer ... to succeed for the sake, not of the fruits of success, but of success itself. ...There is the joy of creating, of getting things done, or simply of exercising one's energy and ingenuity." (*Mapping the Entrepreneurial Psyche*, Inc. Magazine, August 2007)

Although there is no single set of skills and characteristics needed to succeed as an entrepreneur, those commonly cited include perseverance, high-achievement needs, marketplace sensitivity, networking, effective communications, goal setting and calculated risk taking. Entrepreneurial characteristics will be discussed in depth later in the book. At that time, you will assess yourself on these qualities.

One quality we'll look at here in more detail is risk taking. Although entrepreneurs are often considered to be risk takers, research shows they tend to be calculated risk takers rather than high risk takers. Calculated risk takers carefully assess their odds of succeeding and take the necessary steps to do so.

At first glance, the risks of starting a business may seem great. Upon closer scrutiny, however, the risks associated with depending on someone else for one's livelihood prompt many to take the entrepreneurial leap. This is particularly true in today's volatile economic environment. Nascent entrepreneurs frequently see a greater security in depending upon themselves and their own skills and abilities than on an employer. The financial security they feel they can achieve coupled with the desire to be one's own boss—the reasons entrepreneurs most frequently give for starting their own businesses—often tip the scale in favor of entrepreneurship.

Pause and Reflect: Employee/Entrepreneur	
Compare the advantages and disadvantages of being both an employee and an entrepreneur by answering the following questions:	
Employee	**Entrepreneur**
1. What are the financial benefits? *Guaranteed Annual Pay, Not $ investment.*	1. What are the financial benefits? *Pay Control*
2. What are the short and long-term financial risks? *Nothing short-term Possibly long-term*	2. What are the short and long-term financial risks? *Short-term Investment, Possible flop.*
3. What are the emotional rewards?	3. What are the emotional rewards? *Making Something for Yourself.*
4. What are the emotional risks? *Having A bad boss, Work Environment, etc...*	4. What are the emotional risks? *Failure*

Only you can determine whether or not the benefits of pursuing an entrepreneurial future outweigh the risks.

"Information is the key to overcoming fear."

Entrepreneurial Clips
- Carol left her job with a major advertising and public relations firm to start her own public relations firm.
- Hector started his own remodeling company after years in the home construction industry.

Entrepreneurs may be at the helm of either small or large businesses. Although many entrepreneurs start out with the intent of having small businesses, after learning the ropes of entrepreneurship and experiencing success, many raise their aspirations for their businesses.

COMPETITIVE ADVANTAGE
A competitive advantage is gained by offering consumers greater value, increasing the ratio of benefits to price. Such a competitive advantage may stem from the unique or hard-to-find skills and talents you possess that the marketplace needs. This advantage provides a solid foundation on which to build your business.

A business's competitive advantage may come from its ability to offer a unique or hard-to-find product or to deliver it more efficiently and effectively than competitors. Or it can stem from its ability to reach a niche market or provide exemplary customer service. All of these can differentiate a business from the competition and work to its advantage in the marketplace.

Critical Success Factors
Consider marketplace superstars such as Apple® Computer, Coca-Cola®, Starbucks®, and Walmart, to name a few. What competitive advantage does each have? If you thought of things like unique or quality products, excellent customer service, convenient locations, effective marketing, or a fair value exchange for your dollar, you are right on track. These are **Critical Success Factors (CSFs).**

CSFs vary by type of business. For example, speed in product preparation may be a CSF for a coffee shop but not for an upscale restaurant where patrons expect a leisurely dining experience. Location may be a CSF for a print shop but isn't as important for an accountant

Winners in the marketplace, in general, and in your field, in particular, can tell you what customers value. Winners can tell you what sells and what doesn't—what benefits customers are seeking and what features provide them.

In a television interview several year ago, Herb Kelleher, co-founder of Southwest Airlines, attributed their success to their business model—low prices, better service, and an atmosphere of fun. Even though Southwest introduced this model into the airline industry decades ago, Kelleher also commented that no other airline had duplicated it. The question to you is, "Why not?" Why don't businesses learn from others' successes?

Successful companies have figured out what the CSFs are for their types of businesses and made sure they provide them. Now is your opportunity to do the same in the Pause and Reflect activity which follows.

> **Pause and Reflect: Critical Success Factors**
> Carefully consider the type of business you are contemplating. What are the CSF's for this type of business?

Note: Asking you about Critical Success Factors here will help you stay alert to such factors as you work through the activities of this course. If you can't answer the Pause and Reflect question above, revisit it at the end of the course and answer it then.

Too often, aspiring entrepreneurs claim they will have a competitive advantage—lower prices, higher quality, better service—but these claims ring false or are short lived unless they are supported by specific expertise or areas of excellence.

Intellectual Property
Your intellectual property may be the source of your competitive advantage and, perhaps, the most valuable asset of your business. It may include an innovative product, trade secrets, or copyrighted materials. It may be the strong brand you create or the name recognition your business builds.

If your intellectual property is an important asset of your business, consider how you can protect it, just as you would protect any of your business's assets. The following is a brief overview of common methods of protecting intellectual property. Be sure to consult an attorney knowledgeable in the field about how to best deal with your business's intellectual property.

- **Copyright**—protects the creator's exclusive right to control the distribution of an original work of authorship usually for a limited time. As a result of the Berne Convention Implementation Act in 1989, copyright is automatic. Not registering your copyright with the United States Copyright Office, however, may result in reduced damages for infringement. For more information, go to the U.S. Copyright Office at http://www.copyright.gov/.

- **Trade secret**—is a process, formula, pattern, practice, design, instrument, or compilation of information not generally known or reasonably ascertainable that may provide an economic advantage to a business. The classic example of a trade secret is the formula for Coca-Cola, which the company has gone to extraordinary lengths to protect. It is said that only two employees ever know the formula for Coca Cola at the same time. Luckily, such precautions are usually not necessary. Precautions such as marking materials as "confidential" and limiting access to them based on a "need-to-know" basis may be sufficient in some instances. A non-disclosure agreement may also be important.

- **Patent**—is a set of exclusive rights granted to an inventor for a specific time period. The invention must be new, inventive, and useful or industrially applicable. Rights granted to a patentee in most countries prevent others from making, using, selling, offering to sell, or importing the invention. For more information, go to the U.S. Government Patent and Trademark Office's Web site at www.uspto.gov.

- **Trademark**—protects the owner's use of a mark that distinguishes a good or service from others. For more information, go to the U.S. Patent and Trademark Office at www.uspto.gov.

- **Logo**—is a graphical element that, together with its logotype (a uniquely set and arranged typeface), forms a trademark or commercial brand. For more information, call 800-786-9199 or go to the Web site for the U.S. Patent & Trademark Office at www.uspto.gov.

In the case of copyrights and trademarks, you may be able to register them yourself. With patents, you will want to contact an intellectual property attorney although you may want to conduct preliminary research yourself.

Defending infringement violations can be time consuming and costly. In some situations, the costs of enforcing intellectual property rights through litigation outweigh the remedies you might receive. In such instances, the best defense you have against competitors is to offer the highest quality products and best customer service in the marketplace.

Other legal protections that may be helpful to some entrepreneurs are non-disclosure and non-compete agreements.

- **Non-disclosure (confidentiality) agreement**—protects against a person revealing confidential company information, such as customer data, inventions, and trade secrets. Contact an attorney about the likelihood of a non-disclosure agreement affording any real protection.

> **Insight or Common Sense**
> Entrepreneurs often want to ask those with whom they share their business plan to sign a non-disclosure agreement. Some people who are in positions where they work with scores of entrepreneurs or read many business plans will not sign such documents for fear of being erroneously accused of being in breach of such an agreement.

- **Non-compete agreement**—restricts a person's ability to pursue a similar profession or trade in competition against another party (usually the employer). To be enforceable, these agreements typically include a specific time period and geographic location.

Even with adequate protection, it is important to remember that it is not the business idea that leads to success, but the perseverance to follow your dreams and the implementation of your business with excellence.

> *"Opportunity is missed by most people because it is dressed in overalls and looks like work."*
> Thomas Edison

MOTIVATION

For many, the main motivation for starting their own business is to avoid returning to the corporate world. This desire may be precipitated by downsizing from a job or an unsatisfactory job-seeking experience. Businesses they start frequently relate to what they know—previous work or hobbies.

This was the case with Anita. When she was downsized from a large company, her initial thoughts were to return to the corporate world. Even though she was encouraged by friends to enroll in the business startup course that was available as part of her severance package, she had no interest in having her own business. But after months of looking for employment, Anita came to realize that self-employment was her best, if not only, option. Capitalizing on her strong planning and organizational skills, she contracted her services to seminar companies and corporation where she helped plan and set up events and acted as an on-site person when events were held. She remains self-employed today, over a decade later.

For those with a long-standing desire to own their own business, the business they choose may be secondary to the opportunity to act entrepreneurially. The businesses they start may be different from the ones in which they have worked since owning their own business is the primary motivator, rather than owning a particular type of business. Such was the case for the founders of Licorice International, the entrepreneurs featured at the end of Chapter 13, who made a concerted search for a product to sell. This led them into a whole new line of work and industry, the candy industry.

Some workers see having their own businesses as a way to augment full-time job income. Many would really like to own their own business, but, because of financial obligations or high security needs, they can't bring themselves to quit their full-time jobs. They start their businesses while still holding a job, working evenings and weekends until they gain the confidence that their new businesses will support them. These businesses are typically related to what they know—their full-time employment or an avid hobby.

Older workers, particularly those retired or approaching retirement, are frequently interested in starting businesses to supplement their retirement incomes. For them, businesses with low start-up costs, which afford considerable work flexibility, are most desirable. Many Web-based or service businesses provide entrepreneurs considerable control over when and where they work with minimal investment. (*BoomerPreneur: How Baby Boomers Can Start Their Own Business, Make Money and Enjoy Life*, M.B. Izard)

ENTRY STRATEGIES

Once the type of business you wish to start is identified, there are a number of ways to actually get the business started. Starting a business from scratch is the entry strategy first considered by many aspiring entrepreneurs. For some businesses, this is the only entry strategy. But for many others, options include buying an existing business or entering into a licensing or franchising arrangement. For example, if you plan to start a payroll service, you might find that you can purchase an existing service or enter into a franchise agreement to start a payroll service.

There are pluses and minuses to each entry strategy. In a franchise situation, a plus is assistance with the startup process, valuable training, and guidance made available to the entrepreneur. Minuses include the franchise and royalty fees you pay.

There are many types of franchises available. Research is needed to ferret out the one that meets your needs. Talking to other franchisees, including those NOT recommended by the franchisor, as well as consulting the appropriate legal and financial experts, will help you determine if a particular franchise is right for you.

Buying an existing business may provide you many of the same benefits as a franchise—name recognition, established procedures, customers, suppliers, financial data, and so on—without the franchise fee. One key question to determine before buying is why the entrepreneur is selling the business. In addition to asking the seller what their reasons are, talk to customers, vendors, landlords, and others in the industry.

Obtaining the licensing rights to sell another company's products or services is another entry strategy that allows you to sell branded or patented products for a fee. Conversely, licensing your products to others is a way for you to increase sales into new markets.

Insight or Common Sense
Do your due diligence before entering into a franchise or licensing agreement or buying an existing business. Verifying the information provided and conducting your own research is the key to making an informed decision.

WHAT MAKES A BUSINESS RIGHT FOR YOU?
To decide whether or not a business is a good fit for you, you need to first determine whether or not it capitalizes on your strengths, interests, and passions as well as meets your personal and professional goals.

Strengths
Everyone has innate abilities that enable them to do some things better and more easily than others things. When your work utilizes these abilities, you accomplish more while expending less energy than if you were not accessing these strengths.

Following is a simple exercise to demonstrate how utilizing natural abilities enables you to perform better while expending less energy.

Pause and Reflect: Natural vs. Learned
Write your name three times on the lines below.
- _Grant_
- _Grant_
- _Grant_

Using the opposite hand, write your name three more times.
- _Grant_
- _Grant_
- _Grant_

Now answer the questions that follow:
- How did it feel using your opposite hand? _Slow, weak, difficult._

- How well did you write your name with your opposite hand? _Not very well._

- Was it easier the last time you wrote your name using your opposite hand than the first? _No, because I tried to do it faster._
- Even with practice, will you write with your opposite hand as well and easily as you do with the hand you use naturally? _NO_

- How might you apply what you learned in this activity to starting and growing your own business? _Use your best hand._

As an entrepreneur, it's important to be aware of your strengths. It's also important to be aware that you will need to access the talents and strengths of others to shore up your weak areas and build the company you desire.

Passion

Through examining your skills, talents, and successes, you will uncover your own strengths and natural abilities, which will guide you in identifying a business idea for which you are well suited. But strengths are not the only personal factor to consider. What type of business can you truly become excited about starting? What type of business would make work seem like play?

When discussing starting a business with others, you will often hear that you need to "find your passion." This sounds great, but many people are not sure what their "passion" is. Remember Jack Palance in the movie *City Slickers*, as he admonished Billy Crystal to find the "One Thing" in his life that gave it meaning. When asked what the "One Thing" was, Jack Palance responded wisely that each person had to find it for himself. The same is true of finding your business passion.

Through reflecting on your personal history, what you have enjoyed and valued in the past, as well as looking at how you spend your time and money today, you will get an idea of what your "One Thing" might be—what gives your life meaning.

According to Farrah Gray, an entrepreneur who made his first million dollars at age 15 and the author of the book, *Reallionaire, Nine Steps to Becoming Rich from the Inside Out*, successful entrepreneurship stems from defining your area of excellence. He suggests that potential entrepreneurs ask themselves the following questions to identify their passion and an idea for a business:

- What comes easy for me and hard for others?
- What work would I do even if I weren't getting paid?
- What can I give back?

> *"A mediocre idea that generates enthusiasm will go further
> than a great idea that inspires no one."*
> Mary Kay Ash

Personal Goals, Professional Goals, and Dreams

The following true story is a compelling example of the power of positive thinking and goal setting in determining one's future.

At the 2000 Summer Olympics in Sydney, Australia, Maurice Greene, the track athlete, was overheard repeatedly saying to himself while preparing for a race, "I'm the fastest man in the world; I'm the fastest man in the world." Maurice Greene's father was being interviewed by a reporter nearby. Upon overhearing Maurice, he said to the reporter, "He's at it again. Maurice has been saying this since he was a little boy."

Maurice Greene obviously had the ability to dream big and visualize his success from a very young age. He was the fastest man alive that year, capturing the Olympic Gold for the 100-meter race.

What are your dreams and goals? In Activity 3.3 in Chapter 12, you are asked to think about your future—what you would like it to be. Owning your own business is a means to achieving that end—the life you want. What does personal and professional fulfillment mean to you? What would you be doing? Enjoying? Accomplishing? What would your lifestyle be?

In the Featured Entrepreneur story that follows this chapter, read how Charlie Adams, growing up in a sharecropper family, fulfilled his lifelong dream of owning a plantation by purchasing the historic Belmont mansion and grounds and turning it into an event venue and bed and breakfast.

Another important consideration as you contemplate taking on the responsibilities of owning your own business, which can be an all-consuming task, is to identify the role you want work to play in your life. Taking a few moments to reflect on this subject can help you determine if entrepreneurship is really for you.

Knowing in advance the balance you wish to have between work and leisure can also help you determine the type of business you wish to start. Some businesses are more demanding than others. For example, a retail business may require long hours and a seven-day work schedule while an online business may provide schedule and location flexibility.

STUDENT WORKBOOK
Complete Activity 0.2 Work-Leisure Balance in Student Workbook pages (included as end of chapter or in separate loose-leaf packet) in which you clarify the balance of work and leisure you desire in your life in the near and distant future.

Financial Goals
Closely aligned to your personal and professional goals are your financial goals. They may significantly impact the type of business you plan to start.

If you're struggling to pay your bills, obviously the financial rewards of the business will be an important consideration. If you have your financial bases covered and are motivated by a desire to have something

> **Financial Goals Provide Decision-Making Guidance**
> Marilyn decided to postpone her plans to start a business when she determined that the candle shop she had contemplated opening in a local strip center would not provide the income she needed to give up her job. Based on this analysis, she decided to wait until she came up with a more profitable business idea.

interesting and challenging to do, the potential financial rewards will not play as significant a role in choosing a business to start.

Whatever your financial goals for the business, remember that money is the means to an end—the life you want—not an end in itself. With that said, however, it is important that you feel the financial rewards of having your own business are a sufficient return on your investment of dollars, time, and energy. In "Financial Goals Provide Decision-Making Guidance," read how the lack of financial rewards changed one entrepreneur's mind about a particular business idea.

In Activity 3.4 in Chapter 12, you identify your financial goals as well as what assets you have available to invest in your business.

STEP 0: INTRODUCTION TO FEATURED ENTREPRENEUR
Read how Charlie Adams' lifelong dream of owning a plantation resulted in a competitive advantage for his event hosting and catering business.

Featured Entrepreneur Charlie Adams
Belmont Events and Bed and Breakfast

Charlie Adams now owns the keys to the castle, or plantation, that is. Growing up in a sharecropper family, Charlie used to envision the lives of those inside the magnificent homes on the plantations for which his family worked.

Years later he decided to act on his dream and **"do it, rather than just wish I had done it."** He purchased the historic Belmont mansion and grounds, a paragon of architectural talent and fine materials less than 20 miles from Greensboro, North Carolina. Although not for sale at the time of his visit, Charlie left his business card

for the owner in case the property became available. Shortly thereafter, he received a call that it was for sale. His initial challenge was to restore the vintage mansion and its ten acres of shaded and landscaped grounds to the splendor of its past.

The ladies' lunches, initially offered to local patrons, eventually grew into a full-service wedding and event venue booked most weekends of the year for up to 200 guests. Among Belmont's complete services are in-house catering, florists, and overnight lodgings as a part of its Bed and Breakfast, giving visitors a taste of the southern charm of yesteryear and providing **a competitive advantage** in the marketplace.

Not only did Charlie's dream of owning a plantation home take root in his early years, he began acquiring the skills needed to own a successful wedding and event venue early in life as well. As a teen, Charlie learned the hotel and catering business by working at a local hotel. His financial expertise came from years in the corporate world as a financial manager and treasurer for an entertainment association. Bringing in a partner with a background in the entertainment industry helped round out the expertise needed for the business.

Charlie's advice to others contemplating starting their own business is, **"Be prepared for an adventure that nothing else comes close to and memories that you'll treasure for years."** For more information, go to www.belmontevents.com

0.2 activity
work-leisure balance

Directions

On the work-leisure continuum below, "work" indicates working approximately 40+ hours a week with leisure activities restricted to evenings and weekends. "Leisure" represents spending all of your time devoted to areas of personal interests and fulfillment with no earned income. Points in between reflect varying combinations of the two.

On the first continuum, place an "X" at the point on the continuum that represents the balance of work and leisure you have **now**. If you are working full time, the "X" will be all the way to the left.

On the second, third, and fourth continuums, place an "X" at the point on the continuum that represents the balance of work and leisure you would like to have within the next five years, 6-10 years, and 11 or more years. Then answer the questions that follow.

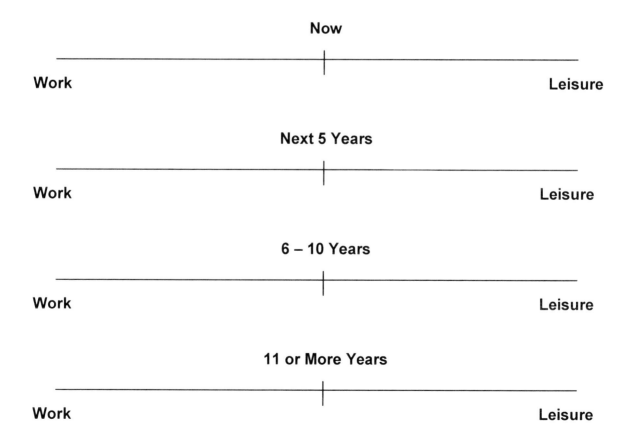

Now

Work   Leisure

Next 5 Years

Work   Leisure

6 – 10 Years

Work   Leisure

11 or More Years

Work   Leisure

a. What changes need to occur for you to move from where you are on the "Now" continuum to where you would like to be on the "Next 5 Years" continuum?

b. What changes need to occur for you to move from where you are on the "Next 5 Years" continuum to where you would like to be on the "6–10 Years" continuum?

c. What changes need to occur for you to move from where you are on the "6–10 Years" continuum to where you would like to be on the "11 or More Years" continuum?

Step 1

Looking Internally —
Your "Acres of Diamonds"

Step 1 Objective

To identify possible business ideas through
- Analyzing current and previous work experiences.
- Examining personal hobbies and interests.
- Evaluating education and skills.

Chapter 3

Sources of Ideas: Work Experience

SOURCES OVERVIEW

Ideas for businesses come from many different sources, as shown in Diagram 1.1. At the top of the list is work experience. Entrepreneurs cite work experience as the avenue used to launch their own businesses more than any other. Through work, nascent entrepreneurs acquire the knowledge and develop the skills they subsequently use in their own businesses. Some are able to identify needs and gaps in the marketplace that their current employer is not addressing; others recognize emerging trends that represent opportunities to the alert entrepreneur.

Sources of Ideas
Work experience
Hobbies and interests
Education, skills, and talents
Marketplace needs
Family, friends, acquaintances
Creativity/Innovation

Diagram 1.1

Work Experience. For experienced workers, their intellectual capital, accumulated from years in the workplace, is likely their most valuable resource. Starting businesses that capitalizes on their experiences often enables them to grow their businesses rapidly and efficiently.

Younger people with limited work experience or unemployed workers, if they have been out of the workforce for some time, may need to focus on other sources of business ideas. Analyzing their hobbies, interests, or educational backgrounds may be a more productive avenue to business ownership. Such was the case with Rhonda, who had not held a job outside of the home in over a decade. At her brother's suggestion—that others would appreciate her gardening and landscaping training and talents—she started her own landscaping business.

Hobbies and Interests. In exploring ideas, it's important to keep in mind that not just any idea will do. What captivates you? Makes you excited to get up in the morning? What would you like to do even if you weren't getting paid for it? What idea can you be passionate about? Personal hobbies and interests are a good starting point to help you uncover the answers to these questions.

Passion for your business can sustain you through the many challenges of business ownership. For some, especially those who have not had the opportunity to try different things and explore their interests and talents, identifying a passion is its own challenge. Working through the activities in this book will help you uncover or clarify what you enjoy and do well.

"Do what you love and the money will follow."

Education, Skills, and Talents. By this stage of your life, you have had a minimum of twelve years in an academic setting exploring your aptitudes, developing skills, and acquiring knowledge. Reflecting on these years, as well as time you've spent honing skills outside of an academic setting, can illuminate strengths and be the launching point of your entrepreneurial future.

Entrepreneur Susan Davidson, featured at the end of Chapter 5, found the language skills she developed through courses in high school and college and later in a Spanish immersion program in Mexico, laid the foundation for her consulting business, working with foreign executives and their families moving to the United States.

Marketplace Needs. A winning business idea satisfies a market need, plain and simple. In other words, the marketplace determines whether or not a business idea is a winner.

If entrepreneurs were able to look into a crystal ball of the future to see what products customers would buy and what industries would flourish, they would all succeed. Without such mystical insights, however, entrepreneurs are confined to less glamorous approaches of analyzing trends, studying the marketplace, and becoming careful observers of human behavior.

Rapid changes in technology today, with their corresponding disruption, renovation, and transformation of the marketplace, exemplify the theory of "creative destruction" espoused by early economist Joseph Shumpeter. He observed that the same innovation that creates opportunity for one business destroys another. In the early 1900s, mass production in factories almost eliminated local dress and shoe shops, and cars replaced the horse and buggy. Today, years after the concept of creative destruction was first identified, emerging industries and fledgling ventures continue to capitalize on the process. Record stores, camera film manufacturers, and pay phones are all but extinct. What technological changes caused these declines?

Technology is just one factor that creates market opportunities; demographic, social, and economic changes account for more. If you don't yet have an idea for your business, you can start with the marketplace and identify what is needed now and what is likely to be needed in the not-so-distant future. If you already have an idea, this is a good time to analyze the marketplace for confirmation that your business idea fills a need. Either way, it's all about the marketplace.

> *"The way to make money is to go find a customer with a problem,*
> *solve it, and sell him the solution."*
> Ed Zimmer, author

Family, Friends, and Others. Many individuals rely heavily upon their informal network of family, friends, colleagues, and professional contacts during the concept development and early start-up stages of their businesses. These individuals are an excellent source of new ideas as they share their marketplace observations and insights. They are also a source of feedback for the ideas you have. This network becomes even more critical as the business is launched. Entrepreneurs access their networks to obtain start-up funds, reach customers, hire staff, and identify sources of business expertise.

Creativity/Innovation. Reorganizing and reconfiguring objects and information in new and innovative ways enables some entrepreneurs to introduce breakthrough products to the marketplace.

Yet the majority of businesses succeed by providing proven products and services to customers efficiently and effectively. Tapping into their own creativity to improve upon what is currently available is one way entrepreneurs can set their businesses apart from the competition.

YOUR ACRES OF DIAMONDS

In Step 1, you analyze your past work experiences, education, and personal interests to identify potential business ideas that capitalize on your natural abilities and strengths. The following story, *Acres of Diamonds*, illustrates the importance of looking at yourself first to identify your entrepreneurial diamond—a winning business idea. The story has been told to hundreds of thousands over the past century, originating with Dr. Russell Herman Conwell, founder of Temple University in Philadelphia, Pennsylvania. Dr. Conwell, an American minister, writer, and lawyer based the story on one shared by a guide he hired to accompany him down the Tigris River in 1870. Reportedly a true story, it goes like this.

In ancient Persia, a farmer grew wearier by the day working his land as rumors reached him of the discovery of diamonds so valuable that a handful could purchase a whole country. Determined to seek his fortune, he sold his farm and for the rest of his life, he traveled the continent in search of diamonds. He found none. Poor, hungry, in rags and despair, he flung himself into the sea.

Crossing a small stream, the man who bought the farmer's property spied a black stone whose prism-like reflections exhibited the colors of the rainbow. He took it to his home and placed it on the mantel. He liked looking at it.

Time passed and a visitor saw the beautiful stone and was awestruck. "Do you know what you've found?" the visitor excitedly asked. Together they rushed to the stream, and stirring the sand they found other gems, more beautiful than the first. The creek bottom was full of them.

Thus, was discovered the great diamond mine of Galconda, the most magnificent diamond mine in the world. The first farmer had owned it but sold it for pennies to look for diamonds elsewhere.

The thing about this story that so profoundly affected Dr. Conwell and, subsequently, millions of others who have heard it over the years is the idea that each of us is, at this moment, standing in the middle of his or her own acres of diamonds.

Your "acres of diamonds" consist of your work experiences, skills, talents and interests. This is where you will likely find your entrepreneurial diamond—an idea for a successful business. Tim Barnes, entrepreneur and visiting lecturer at the Centre for Entrepreneurship at University College London, emphasized this point when he said, "One thing that successful ideas have in common is that they are based on some form of expertise, prior knowledge or experience, or a combination of all three." For more on the topic, see "What makes a good business idea?" Cambridge University. http://www.cue.org.uk/files/training-day-tim-barnes.pdf

Now you will start the idea exploration process by looking carefully at current and previous work experiences and the skills you learned along the way.

WORK EXPERIENCES

Work experience is the number-one source of ideas for starting a business for anyone, young or old. But the older you are, the more likely you are to have extensive and valuable work experience.

Some entrepreneurs capitalize on what they learned working for others and either copy or slightly modify products or services their previous or current employer offers in the marketplace. Others offer products or services similar to what their employer offers but to different markets, often focusing on small or underserved niche markets that their employer does not pursue. This latter strategy, of targeting smaller markets, fits both the budget and the competitive abilities of many new businesses. Read how this strategy worked for one entrepreneur in "Logoed Shirts."

> **Logoed Shirts**
> When her employer, a producer of Hawaiian-style shirts, decided to stop producing logoed sports team and corporate shirts because they took too much time away from his core business, Hawaiian shirts, Ariel decided this was the business for her. Her new custom shirts company caters to the needs of local sports teams and corporations in this niche market.

Now take a few moments to reflect upon your work experience.

Pause and Reflect: Work
Answer the following questions to help you identify entrepreneurial opportunities that build on your current or previous work and industry experiences:
1. Do customers complain of a problem that my current or previous employer does not address?

2. Can I save customers money by doing things slightly differently than my employer?

3. Can I develop a product or service to complement those offered by my employer?

4. What other markets—those not currently being reached—exist for my employers' products or services?

5. Is the market growing at such a rate that it offers an opportunity for new entrants into the field?

In many of the Snapshots and Featured Entrepreneur stories throughout this book, you will read how work experience played a significant role in the businesses these entrepreneurs started and the success of these businesses. In some cases, the business directly related to previous jobs, as was the case with Dave Polny, whose classic car restoration business dated back to his first job in a car repair shop. In other cases, entrepreneurs like Delena Stout of Brookside Barkery and Bath, who you will read about later in Chapter 10, commented that almost everything she had ever done in previous jobs helped prepare her for her entrepreneurial venture.

Snapshot of Entrepreneur
David Polny was able to utilize previous work experiences to turn his passion for classic cars into a restoration business, 190 SL Services.

Civilian life after a 20-year military career allows Dave to do what others only dream of doing—restoring vintage automobiles to their original splendor. His business, 190 SL Services, specializes in full and partial restorations, servicing and repairing vintage, classic and muscle cars with a specialty in Mercedes Benz 190 SL. Located in Aberdeen, North Carolina, the business offers a full show-quality restoration that could start as high as

David Preston's "Best of Show," The International 190 SL Group Concours d'Elegance
Lexington, KY - September 8, 2007

$170,000 to $225,000, depending on the vehicle. Dave's business has attained worldwide recognition and is reached primarily through his Web site at www.190slservices.com.

Dave worked on and around cars for many years. At the young age of 13 while working at a garage on Saturdays, he learned a valuable lesson from the business's owner which he uses to this day—to rebuild rather than replace.

Dave says his years in Special Operations as a Green Beret helped prepare him for life as an entrepreneur. In both situations, he explained, you need to be able to think on your feet and take initiative.

Upon leaving the military, Dave connected with the Entrepreneur Center at Sandhills Community College, where he received help developing his plans for starting a business. When the classic car restoration business for which Dave subcontracted work became available to buy, he partnered with a customer of the business to purchase it.

In identifying business opportunities, it's helpful to look at your work experience from a broad perspective. Not only look at present and previous jobs, but also at what you learned about your industry and the contacts you made along the way.

Student Workbook
Complete Activity 1.1, 360-Degree Perspective, Present and Previous Work Experience in Student Workbook pages. Before you start this Activity, in which you are asked to brainstorm ideas, consider the rules of brainstorming shown here.

Brainstorming

* Accept all ideas (briefly list all).

* Withhold evaluation.

* Build on others' ideas.

Remember, More is better!

Throughout this book you will be asked to continue your brainstorming activities. Why brain-storm? Brainstorming does the following:
* *Encourages creativity and expands one's thinking on a topic.*
* *Produces many ideas*
* *Encourages individuals to be open-minded.*
For the purposes of brainstorming, you should list a minimum of five responses; seven or more would be even better.

In some jobs your work may be very specific and narrowly defined, while in other jobs you are exposed to outside organizations and people who enrich your knowledge and provide valuable contacts for the future. In the following section, Industry Opportunities, you take the broad view and consider how your work relates to both your industry and marketplace.

INDUSTRY OPPORTUNITIES

In the workplace, typically you not only learn a job, you also learn an industry. You know how your industry works and its support systems. This knowledge may very well enable you to identify business opportunities that exist at different levels within your industry's distribution chain. See Diagram 1.2 for common distribution chains.

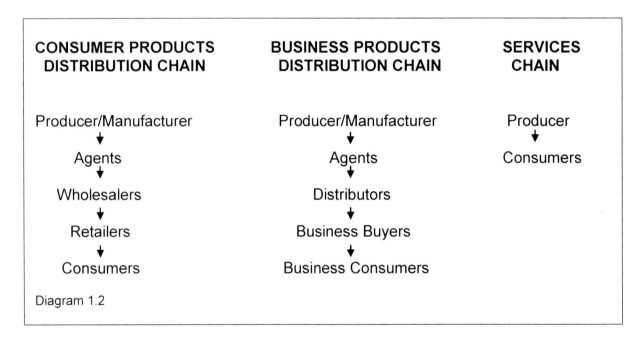

CONSUMER PRODUCTS DISTRIBUTION CHAIN	BUSINESS PRODUCTS DISTRIBUTION CHAIN	SERVICES CHAIN
Producer/Manufacturer	Producer/Manufacturer	Producer
↓	↓	↓
Agents	Agents	Consumers
↓	↓	
Wholesalers	Distributors	
↓	↓	
Retailers	Business Buyers	
↓	↓	
Consumers	Business Consumers	

Diagram 1.2

Vertical Laddering. Start by looking at the typical chain of distribution within the industry in which you work. Steps likely include producing, packaging, selling, and transporting the product along the path from producer to customer. Value is added at each of these steps.

The consumer and business products distribution chains typically have multiple levels, as shown in Diagram 1.2. In some industries, one level within the chain performs multiple functions and, therefore, the chain is much shorter. The service distribution chain is one such chain. Often the producer (service provider) produces and delivers the service, working directly with the customer. There may be no intermediary steps.

In Activity 1.2 in the Student Workbook, you will be asked to look at the entire distribution system for your industry, where you fit into it, and what other opportunities exist as a result of your industry knowledge and experience.

The Internet has dramatically altered the way some products are distributed, flattening the distribution process and creating exciting opportunities for astute entrepreneurs. Many entrepreneurs are now able to offer their products directly to customers. Producers can reach millions by having their own Web sites or going through online vendors. The book industry is a good example of this. Many writers no longer sell through publishers but reach consumers directly through their own Web sites or through online sellers such as Amazon and Barnes and Noble.

Following are several examples of how moving from one rung to another within an industry's distribution chain provided workers opportunities to become entrepreneurs. We'll use the term "vertical laddering" to describe this movement up or down the distribution chain.

Example: Movement within the Consumer Products Distribution Chain

A store manager moved up the consumer products distribution chain to become a manufacturer's representative and sell the products he previously purchased. This person's knowledge of the products and industry enabled him to start his own business and move from the retail to the wholesale level.

Example: Movement within the Business Products Distribution Chain

A teacher started her own business selling educational materials to school districts and other teachers as an independent sales representative for a publisher of textbooks, test materials, and reading programs. She moved from being a consumer on the business products distribution chain to the agent level. As a teacher, she had used a variety of educational products that were sold to her school district. Her knowledge of these products and the distribution system enabled her to make this transition.

Example: Movement within the Services Distribution Chain

The research director in charge of drug testing for a large pharmaceutical company started her own pharmaceutical consulting and drug testing company. Her first client was her former employer.

Contracting services back to former employers can be an excellent business entry strategy, as employers may be happy to subcontract work to former employees who are competent and left their jobs on good terms.

In another example of movement within the services chain, an information technology (IT) manager for a large company, who hired many IT consultants to augment his company's in-house IT work force, utilized this experience to start his own IT consulting firm. His new company provided IT staff to companies such as the one for which he previously worked. Thus he became of provider of IT services instead of a consumer of these services. Read more about this entrepreneur in the Snapshot of Entrepreneur that follows.

Snapshot of Entrepreneur
As a director of global network engineering for a large company, Robert Jewell was frequently in need of talented IT staff. The demand for such skills far outstripped the supply of qualified consultants in his area. As a result, Robert started his own business, Network Integration Services (NIS), an IT consulting firm specializing in the design and deployment of information technology services. Starting primarily in networking, workstations, and servers, NIS later added expertise in electrical engineering, disaster recovery planning, and high availability computing environments. Robert's previous employer was one of his early clients.

By addressing the need for highly skilled labor, Robert has continued to grow his company successfully. He enrolled in a business planning course to learn how to develop a strategic plan for the company's growth. In an industry in which anyone could hang up a shingle, NIS added a level of professionalism by touting its engineering background and focusing on quality.

One commonality among all of these examples is that in each instance, valuable contacts were made both within the business and the industry. These contacts and relationships opened the door for the entrepreneur to transition from their current job to starting their own businesses. In some cases, entrepreneurs sold the products of the businesses with whom they had previously worked; other entrepreneurs sold their products to contacts made through their previous jobs. As the saying goes, "It's all about who you know."

Could you succeed like these entrepreneurs by leveraging your work experience and personal contacts within your industry to start a business?

Horizontal Laddering. This term refers to starting a business by using your work experience and skills in an industry other than the one in which you acquired them. Management skills such as planning, organizing, leading, and controlling are readily transferable from one situation and industry to another. Many who have these skills have a great deal of mobility.

Many technical skills are transferable, as well. This was the case of the medical doctor who acted as a consultant to attorneys in medical malpractice cases. Are there other industries in which you could use your management or technical skills?

Entrepreneurial Clips
- Marco, a police officer, consulted with small businesses on security-related issues.
- Carmina, a college professor teaching management, utilized her considerable teaching experience to develop seminars for a corporate training company.

STUDENT WORKBOOK
Now examine your industry to identify potential business opportunities. Complete Activity 1.2, Industry Analysis and Laddering, in the Student Workbook pages at end of chapter or in separate Student Workbook loose-leaf packet.

1.1   360-degree perspective, present and previous work experiences

Directions. Complete the following.

Present Work Experiences
a. Current or most recent job responsibilities, duties, and activities

b. Skills/talents used in current or most recent job

Past Work Experiences
c. Previous jobs — responsibilities, duties, and activities

d. Skills/talents used in previous jobs

e. I know allot about

f. Brainstorm business ideas that relate to unmet needs or niche markets observed in present and previous jobs. Do not evaluate how feasible or desirable these ideas are at this time.

NOTE: Throughout the activities included in the Student Workbook, you are asked to brainstorm. To do so, write down ideas as they occur, withholding any evaluation of the feasibility or desirability of the ideas at the time. Typically the longer the list of ideas, the more creative the ideas. For purposes of activities in this course, a MINIMUM of 5-7 ideas should be listed when you are asked to brainstorm. **Even though these brainstorming instructions are NOT repeated each time you are asked to brainstorm, these directions apply.**

Synthesis of past and present work experiences

Of the ideas generated in this activity, which three appeal to you the most and why?

	Favorite Idea	Why Idea Appeals to Me
1		
2		
3		

1.2 activity industry analysis and laddering

Industry Analysis

Directions. Now that you have closely examined your work experiences for potential business idea, you will do the same for the industry in which you work(ed). To do so, follow these steps.

Step 1: Distribution Chain. On Diagram 1.1 below, circle the heading that best describes the distribution chain within which you work—"Consumer Products", "Business Products" or "Services." If you are not currently employed, do so for one of your previous jobs.

Note: If your work involves interfacing closely with more than one distribution chain, you may wish to examine each separately by repeating this activity more than once.

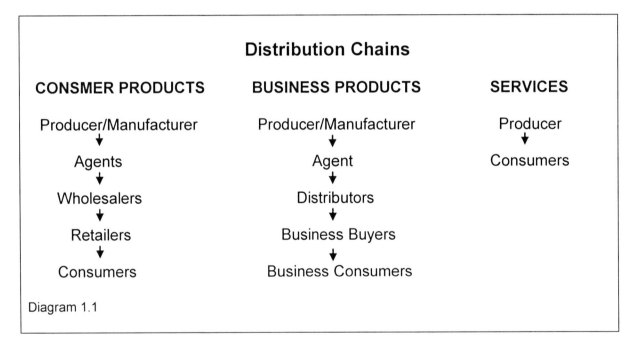

Distribution Chains

CONSMER PRODUCTS	BUSINESS PRODUCTS	SERVICES
Producer/Manufacturer	Producer/Manufacturer	Producer
↓	↓	↓
Agents	Agent	Consumers
↓	↓	
Wholesalers	Distributors	
↓	↓	
Retailers	Business Buyers	
↓	↓	
Consumers	Business Consumers	

Diagram 1.1

Step 2. Rung on Distribution Chain. Within the distribution chain you identified, circle the rung on distribution chain that best describes the level at which you work(ed).

Laddering Vertically

Directions. Now that you have identified your industry's distribution chain and where you fit into it, use this information to identify potential businesses you can start utilizing knowledge of your industry.

1. Business Ideas. Brainstorm businesses you can start by moving up or down the distribution chain in which you worked For example, a store buyer might start a manufacturing representative's agency to sell the products he or she formerly purchased. (More examples are included in textbook.)

2. Contacts Made. List people with whom you frequently interface(ed), both inside and outside the business.

3. How Contacts Can Help. Brainstorm how the individuals listed above may be of assistance to you in starting a business.

Laddering Horizontally

Directions. Now consider other industries that might benefit for your knowledge and skills. For example, a police officer might utilize his/her knowledge of safety and security as a security consultant to businesses.

1. Business Ideas. Brainstorm the types of businesses you could start in which you would perform the <u>same or similar work or offer the same or similar products</u> as what you do now but to totally different industries.

2. Sub-Contracting Possibilities. If you started your own business, could you subcontract your skills back to your present or previous employer? Checkmark answer below.

_____ Yes

_____ No

_____ Not Sure (If you are not sure, how can you find out?)

Synthesis of industry analysis and laddering

Of the ideas generated in this activity, which three appeal to you the most and why?

	Favorite Idea	Why Idea Appeals to Me
1		
2		
3		

Chapter 4

Sources of Ideas:

Hobbies and Interests

Turn something you love doing into a successful business. Now there's an exciting entry strategy. Many craft and hobby enthusiasts do just that. Thousands of sites on the Internet offer information and support on how to do so and enable you to display your wares.

Although this entry strategy may be a good one, enthusiasm must be tempered with a realistic assessment of the commercial feasibility of such an endeavor. Will you be able to produce and sell enough to make your business financially worthwhile? Are there enough potential buyers to make the business profitable?

A major benefit of this entry strategy is that you will be doing something you like or even love. This passion often sustains a person during the challenging early years of a business startup. Also, the experience and expertise you developed during your days as a hobbyist and the contacts you made will be invaluable in your own business.

Technology has done a great deal to encourage the trend of turning hobbies into businesses by providing an avenue for hobbyists to sell their

> **Hobby and Work, Winning Combo**
> Lee, a gourmet cook and professional nurse, combined her knowledge of nutrition and health with her skills in the kitchen to start a food preparation business aimed at customers with special dietary needs.

wares on the Internet. For as little as $10 for a domain name and a nominal fee for a Web hosting service, you can open shop, so to speak. Online craft stores and eBay® are other avenues.

Consider not only the hobby itself, but everything that surrounds it. For example, if you love gardening, business possibilities may include becoming a distributor of gardening supplies, teaching classes on gardening, caring for floral and plant displays in corporate office buildings, or writing a gardening book. In Activity 1.2 in the previous chapter, where you examined vertical and horizontal laddering, you did a similar thing for work experiences.

Insight or Common Sense
For IRS purposes, certain criteria must be met for a hobby to qualify as a business. Whether or not there is a profit motive is one. Check with your attorney or accountant for guidance on this issue.

One challenge of turning a hobby into a business is to balance the passion for the hobby aspect of it with the need to devote adequate time and energy to the entrepreneurial side—planning, marketing, bookkeeping, and finance.

Pause and Reflect: Hobbies
Answer the following questions.
- Do I have an interest in turning any of my hobbies into a business?

- If so, would I be able to *produce* enough to have a successful business?

- If so, would I be able to *sell* enough to have a successful business?

Snapshot of Entrepreneurs
Capitalizing on the experience they gained through personal remodeling projects and building several homes for themselves, Sara and Rhasad began building homes as a sideline to other full-time jobs. They contracted out many basic home building tasks, then moved into the home and finished all the detail work, such as woodworking and painting. They lived in the home for two to three years while they completed the project and began work on their next home. Once the next home was inhabitable, they would sell the home they lived in and start the process again.

Upon their retirement, home building became a full-time project for the couple. Although this type of enterprise is not for everyone, it allowed Sara and Rhasad to use their skills and talents to augment their income.

Entrepreneurial Clips
- Susan turned her quilting hobby into a quilting services and supply shop.

- Mike grew his hobby of making mission-type wood furniture into a business as a specialty furniture producer, selling through designers and retailers.
- Jordan's love of bicycling propelled him to start a retail bike shop specializing in equipment and clothing for cyclists.
- Tyrone's hobby of building wood chests indirectly led him to start an engraving business. After experiencing difficulty in finding someone to engrave the small brass plates he attached to the front of his wood chests, he identified an opportunity to do engraving for others. He specializes in engraving trophies and plaques for businesses and schools.
- Rachel's love of dance and years of experience led to the opening of her own dance studio.
- April, who enjoyed making gift baskets, found that her hobby took over her life to the point that, after three years of conducting business on the side, she quit her day job. She markets her baskets at craft fairs and in gift shops in nearby resort communities.

One of the caveats of turning a hobby or personal interest into a business is that your passion may become a job. Then what will you do for fun and recreation?

STUDENT WORKBOOK
Complete Activity 1.3, 360-Degree Perspective, Hobbies, Interests, Passions, and Pastimes.

1.3

activity
360-degree perspective, hobbies, interests, passions, and pastimes

Hobbies and Interests

a. Things I like to do — hobbies, interests, and pastimes

b. Things I have enjoyed doing in the past

c. Things I am passionate about

d. Skills, talents, or interests that my hobbies and passions utilize

e. What else I like/enjoyed about the hobbies, interests, and pastimes listed in "a-c."

f. Brainstorm ideas for businesses that relate to your hobbies, interests, passions, and pastimes and/or use the skills and talents you developed in these activities.

Synthesis of hobbies, interests, passions, and pastimes

Of the ideas generated in this activity, which three appeal to you the most and why?

	Favorite Idea	Why Idea Appeals to Me
1		
2		
3		

© Achēve Consulting Inc.

Chapter 5

Sources of Ideas: Education and Skills

Although many of your skills were likely acquired through work experiences, some may be the result of academic coursework, self-study, or trial and error. Perhaps you earned a degree or certificate which allowed you to work in a particular field or you apprenticed with a skilled craftsman. Perhaps you pursued coursework to develop innate talents.

Closely scrutinizing your educational background can help you recognize specific expertise that may be your entrepreneurial admission ticket. Identifying areas where you excelled or in which you were particularly interested can also help you identify businesses which will utilize your strengths. Many years in the classroom may have enabled you to develop expertise and skills that can be marketed to others.

A twist on the strategy described above is to identify the business you want to start and work backwards, acquiring the skills and knowledge you need. You may enroll in courses or look for certain types of work opportunities for preparation. Tony, featured in the textbox "Working Backwards to Go Forward," did both.

> **Working Backwards to Go Forward**
> Someday Tony would like to own his own bakery. Realizing there is more to owning a bakery than his love of baking, Tony enrolled in the culinary arts program at his local community college, where the curriculum included an internship in the field. Completing this internship has enabled Tony to move toward his ultimate goal of opening a bakery.

Angel was another example of working backwards to move forward. After her last child started school, she returned to college to pursue an interior design degree in order to launch her own interior design business. Through an internship, which was a part of her college curriculum, she built ties within the design community and further prepared herself for her eventual business ownership.

"It is possible to fly without motors, but not
without knowledge and skill."
Wilbur Wright

Some skills, such as sales or financial expertise, apply to a broad range of business opportunities. This allows the potential entrepreneur much latitude in the types of businesses to consider. Other skills, such as technical know-how, are narrower in scope and require the entrepreneur to look closely at related areas.

In technical fields, the skills you have today may not be the ones you need tomorrow, so education is a continual process. The need for lifelong learning is necessary for functioning effectively on a personal level, as well, such as using the latest computer software or iPhone.

Perhaps you have taken coursework or developed your own expertise through a lengthy period of trial and error and independent study. Or you may have had the opportunity to work closely with a talented individual who taught you the skills of a trade. There is more than one way to acquire the knowledge and skills you need. Persistence and being open to new information and experiences will enable you to grow into the person you need to become to succeed.

"The great aim of education is not
knowledge but action."
Herbert Spencer

Entrepreneurial Clips
- Ramon capitalized on his degree in horticulture and started his own landscaping business.
- Lindsey's degree in hospitality management and training as a chef prepared her to start her own business as a personal chef.
- Justin started a kitchen design shop utilizing his design background.
- John's training in heating and air conditioning prepared him to open his own heating and air conditioning service, which grew to employ 11 others.

- Tatiana's master's degree in botany motivated her to grow and sell orchids and other exotic plants, both wholesale and retail.

Now you will wrap up Step 1 by carefully examining your educational background for strengths and interests. This concludes the exploration of your personal "Acres of Diamonds," skills, talents, and abilities that will provide you a strong foundation on which to build a successful business.

STUDENT WORKBOOK
Complete Activity 1.4, 360-Degree Perspective, Education, Skills, and Talents, to thoroughly examine your own educational background. After having done so you will have concluded the exploration of your "Acres of Diamonds," the talents that lie in your "own backyard." Then complete Activity 1.5, Step 1—Your Acres of Diamonds, Synthesis of Ideas Generated by Looking Internally, Activities 1.1 – 1.4.

STEP 1: INTRODUCTION TO FEATURED ENTREPRENEUR
Learning foreign languages through classroom studies and international travels helped prepare Susan Davidson to start a consulting business, providing services to foreign managers and their families coming to the United States.

Featured Entrepreneur Susan Davidson
Beyond Borders, Inc.
Executive Coaching and Services

Susan Davidson launched her business, Beyond Borders, Inc., to provide services to help integrate international managers and expatriates and their families into the social and business communities of the United States. Her business quickly grew to include executive coaching and leadership training as well.

Susan's **passionate** interest in the international community began in her youth and motivated her to study French and then participate in a Spanish immersion program as an adult. On any given Saturday night, a dinner party at her home might include guests from Russia, France, Germany, South America, or Kenya. She has traveled extensively, 28 countries in all, studying Spanish in Guatemala and French in the south of France.

A visit with a Service Core of Retired Executives (SCORE) counselor at the Small Business Administration (SBA) helped Susan develop her business idea into a workable plan. Her SCORE counselor, a retired international marketing executive, advised her that a real need/niche was to work with non-Americans to assist them in the otherwise difficult and frustrating process of adapting and integrating into the U.S. community and workplace. He counseled her that most U.S.-based global companies spend the majority of their relocation funds to help American expatriates make the transition into their foreign assignments—but often ignore the needs of in-bound transferees to the United States.

Following several consultations with her SCORE counselor, Susan **conducted an online survey** with 63 international professionals, followed by in-depth one- to two-hour telephone interviews with 32 of the respondents to gain a thorough understanding of the challenges and obstacles they had encountered in their efforts to live and work in the United States.

While learning the intercultural field, Susan spoke with a former corporate colleague who had become a certified executive coach. The colleague encouraged her to investigate coach training programs and become a formally trained coach. As a result, Susan enrolled in a program accredited by the International Coach Federation. Susan's formal training and years of work experience in American corporations gave her credibility in the corporate world and allowed her to speak with knowledge to clients.

To build her coaching practice, Susan **initially offered complimentary sessions** to friends, other new coaches and family members, which gave her the opportunity to practice her coaching skills and build her confidence. When Susan "went public," she let all of her friends and business contacts know that she was offering coaching services and looking for prospective clients.

Susan's business allows her to **fulfill her personal and financial goals** of having freedom and flexibility in her work while at the same time making a comfortable income. This freedom allows time for travel, both domestically and internationally, and for Susan to have control over her day-to-day work/play schedule.

Susan's **advice** to others interested in starting their own business is to

1. **Have a nine-month cash reserve that can sustain you while you develop your business.** Assume you will make zero income for up to nine months. In other words, plan for the worst and hope for the best--but you *must* plan to live on savings or other income for a good part of the year, unless you already have clients when you open your doors.
2. **Already have prospective clients lined up and be ready to make sales calls:** That is, identify, contact and speak with prospective clients on the telephone or face to face about your services and how you might serve their needs. Building your business is a contact sport!
3. **Be visible in building your network and prospective client base.** Marketing (i.e., a Web site, brochure, business cards, articles or speeches, etc.) is not enough. Ultimately, you must sell. The selling process begins when you get to the point where you engage in a one-on-one conversation with a prospective client about how your business services might address that client's needs. To do business, you eventually *must* talk to a person, determine his or her needs and offer a solution (i.e., a detailed discussion, written proposal, or formal presentation).

For more information, go to www.beyondborders.us

1.4 360-degree perspective, education, skills, and talents

Educational Background

a. My favorite subjects in school

b. Why these subjects interested me

c. Skills acquired through formal education

d. Training and skills acquired <u>outside</u> of formal education

e. Skills I would like to strengthen through additional training.

Strengths

f. What I do well NOW

g. What I have done well in the PAST

h. What has resulted in positive recognition and/or awards

i. Skills and talents utilized in activities listed in items "f-h"

j. OTHERS would say my strengths, skills, and talents are

k. Brainstorm a list of ideas for businesses that relate to your educational and personal strengths and talents.

Synthesis of education and skills
Of the ideas generated in this activity, which three appeal to you the most and why?

	Favorite Idea	Why Idea Appeals to Me
1		
2		
3		

1.5 activity, step 1 synthesis, "your acres of diamonds," ideas generated by looking internally, activities 1.1 – 1.4

Directions. Looking back over the ideas identified in each of the Synthesis sections of the four activities included in Step 1, choose the five ideas that appeal to you the most and list them here.

	Favorite Idea	Brief Explanation/ Description	Why Idea Appeals to Me
1			
2			
3			
4			
5			

Step 2

Looking Externally — The Marketplace

Step 2 Objective

To identify possible business ideas through:

- Identifying needs, wants, problems, and trends in the marketplace.
- Applying innovative solutions to existing products/ services or creating new ones.
- Obtaining input from others.

Chapter 6

Identify Wants, Needs, and Gaps

In the previous chapters, you looked inward—at your skills, work experiences, and interests. In the following chapters, you will look outward—at the marketplace, either for a new business idea or for market confirmation that the idea you have is a good one.

Remember the story, "Acres of Diamonds," about a poor farmer in ancient Persia who sold his farm and spent the rest of his life traveling the continent looking for diamonds? Unknowingly, he had sold the largest diamond field in all of Persia and wasted his life looking for diamonds elsewhere.

Had the farmer taken the time to learn what rough diamonds looked like and carefully explored his own property, he would have been wealthy beyond his wildest dreams. Similarly, you will want to know what an entrepreneurial diamonds looks like—what makes a winning business idea.

WINNING BUSINESS IDEAS

A winning business idea satisfies a market need, plain and simple. In other words, the marketplace determines whether or not a business idea is a winner. You have only to look around you to see how the marketplace affects a business's success. An Italian restaurant may thrive in one location but fail dismally in another location in the same city. The surrounding customer base for the latter may be very different and have different food preferences. Home construction in one area of the country may be booming yet stagnate in another area because of poor economic conditions. It's all about the relevant marketplace.

If you don't yet have an idea for a business, a good starting point is to analyze the marketplace and identify what is needed. These observations may be of a *personal* nature—based on your day-to-day experiences while shopping, eating, and participating in local events. Or they may stem from your observations of unfulfilled needs in your current job or industry.

If you already have a business idea, this is a good time to analyze the marketplace to ensure that a need exists for the products or services you plan to offer.

In both instances, the marketplace and how well you meet its needs will determine the success or failure of your business.

MARKETPLACE NEEDS

Since marketplace needs are the diamonds you are seeking, how can you improve your odds of spotting them? The best way is to adopt an entrepreneurial mindset. Entrepreneurs look to solve problems, reach underserved markets, or remedy performance gaps in the marketplace.

Solve a Problem

While some entrepreneurial ideas come from technological breakthroughs, flashes of insights, or revolutionary concepts, the reality is that most ventures are created as a result of entrepreneurs solving problems that exist in the marketplace—frustrations, disappointments, and discomforts of one sort or another. Entrepreneurs see such problems as opportunities.

> **Solve a Problem**
> Upon moving to the United States, Maria experienced difficulty obtaining food items from her native country, Ecuador, and found others did, as well. She started a small retail shop to import and sell these items to others in her community, who, like her, longed for the "taste of home."

Delena Stout, Featured Entrepreneur at the end of Chapter 10, came up with her idea for Brookside Barkery and Bath as a result of the problem she experienced trying to find a place to wash her large dogs. Addressing this problem and capitalizing on consumer interest in healthy, natural, and holistic pet foods, Delena launched

Brookside Barkery and Bath, which has since expanded to include a second location and on-line store.

Entrepreneurial Clips
- Noting the difficulties that two-income families had transporting their children to and from after-school activities, orthodontic appointments, dance lessons and the like, Brooke started an after-school transportation service to meet the needs of this target market.
- Software tailored to meet the strategic planning needs of small to mid-sized companies provided Kyle an edge over the many other management consultants in the field.

Identifying "Points of Pain" is a good way to recognize problem areas, according to entrepreneurship professor, Donna Duffey. She suggests that you consider:
- The complaints you have or those you hear friends and acquaintances make about products and services they purchase.
- Inconveniences you experience when purchasing a product or acquiring a service.
- A product or service "flaw" that is difficult to deal with, such as packaging that takes way too much time to open or instructions that are way too complex for the average buyer to follow.
- Money that seems to be "lost" with little value returned.
- A simpler way to access a product or service (less hassle).
- Something that can make life easier.
- A product or service that can contribute to health or well-being (literally removing pain of one kind or another).

In identifying a solution to a problem, look at the problem in its larger context rather than directly. For example, customer service complaints have decreased significantly for companies which have sought ways to "entertain" customers during their wait times. Techniques range from music and news feeds playing in your ear on the telephone to displaying magazines beside checkout lines. Wait lines designed as mazes give customers an illusion of faster progress while mirrors beside elevator doors distract waiting building tenants. Identifying the problem as customer boredom rather than actual wait time enabled many businesses to reduce customer complaints.

Reach Underserved Markets—Fill a Niche
Large businesses typically focus on mass markets. This provides an opportunity for small business to focus on niche markets. Dave Polny's business, 190 SL Services, featured in Chapter 3, specializes in full and partial restorations and servicing

vintage and classic cars with a specialty of Mercedes Benz 190 SLs. Because this need has not being addressed by mainstream auto service providers, customers come from around the country.

Read "Something for Everyone" for another example of a business fulfilling a niche market.

Fill a Performance Gap

When there is a gap between customers' needs and what is available to them, there is a business opportunity. Many times small businesses, with their close relationships to customers, are able to discern these gaps and are nimble and quick in addressing them. For example, entrepreneur Dr. James Sheehan found that school district administrators in his area were data rich and information poor—

> **Something for Everyone**
> On the extreme end of the niche world of dating sites is MulletPassions.com. Businesses competing with companies such as Match.com or eHarmony are seeing more success targeting those with specific interests; hence sites like Golfmates.com and SingleParent.com.
> "A Dating Site for Everyone" by Ellen McCarty, *The Washington Post.*

DRIP as he referred to it. Even though considerable information was collected regarding school district operations, it was not in a format that could be easily used by school managers. This gap propelled Dr. Sheehan to start his business, Schoolfinances.com, providing systems and reports that present data in a clear and meaningful way to school districts.

Fulfill a Customer Want

Small businesses' close proximity to the customer also gives them a competitive advantage by affording them the opportunity to provide excellent customer service and unique or customized products. For example, Bill and his wife, Vicky, adopted a business strategy for their online motorcycle apparel and accessories business that was different than that of their larger wholesale competitors. As a small business, they realized that sizeable minimum orders created problems for many small business retailers. As a result, they decided not to require a minimum purchase. This enabled them to service small accounts not served by larger suppliers. Their one-stop shopping site for small retailers worked well for them, and their wholesale business grew to 85 percent of their sales before they sold their business to pursue other interests.

There are many techniques to help you spot marketplace problems, niches, and gaps. To do so, you need to raise your antennae to pick up marketplace signals. The following behaviors will help you do so:

- **Listen** to people around you—friends, family, colleagues, customers. What are they saying? Complaining about? What problems are they experiencing?
- **Read** magazines, newspapers, and books, and scan the Internet. What trends are identified? What topics are popular?
- **Observe** the world around you. Read in "Velcro Invention—A Walk in the Park" how engineer George Mesral's observation skills led to the creation of Velcro. Howard Schultz, the founder of Starbucks, is another example of how important observation skills are to entrepreneurial success. On a visit to Milan, Italy, Schultz reportedly noted the social atmosphere in the local coffee shops and later sought to recreate this experience for patrons of his own coffee shops.

Research

Trends, changes in government regulations, and technology innovations are all sources of potential business ideas. Researching these changes and their implications for the marketplace may allow you to anticipate emerging customers' needs.

> **Velcro Invention—
> A Walk in the Park**
> George Mesral, the inventor of Velcro, demonstrated an entrepreneurial mindset as he walked through the woods and noticed how cockleburs became caught in his clothes and in his dog's fur. An engineer by trade, he decided to examine why they stuck so tightly. His observation and investigation led to the development of Velcro.* How many others had the same experience yet failed to see the possibilities in what they observed?
> *The History of VELCRO® and Velcro Products.
> http://www.troyerproducts.com/velcrohistory.asp

Identifying trends early gives entrepreneurs the opportunity to offer their products and services before the competition is strong. Browse the Web to identify trends related to your particular area of interest or industry. For example, if you have an interest in technology, you may want to visit Xconomy.com for technology news and trends. On this Web site, you can view the list of businesses being funded by venture capitalists. To do so, type "venture capital funding" in the Search box. Looking at these businesses can help you anticipate which areas are growing. Similar Web sites exist in other industries.

Keeping a "Journal of Ideas" that solves customers' problems, addresses their unmet needs, or fills product/service gaps in the marketplace is a way to capture and retain ideas as they are identified. It also provides the following benefits:

- You have a place to record your ideas in an organized fashion for future reference and consideration.
- It also teaches you the mindset of looking for opportunities continuously and all around you. This mindset is needed to both start your business and to continually offer innovative products to grow it. Would Apple Computer be as successful as they are if they marketed the same products they did 25 years ago? Successful businesses continually innovate.

Later in this book, you will learn the factors against which items in your "Journal of Ideas" should be assessed.

*"At the center of an opportunity is an idea,
but not all ideas are opportunities."*

Insight or Common Sense
A simple technique like noting products available elsewhere but not in your home community is a way of turning your travels into entrepreneurial adventures.

STUDENT WORKBOOK

To practice identifying potential business opportunities, complete Activity 2.1, Points of Pain; Activity 2.2, Journal of Ideas—Market Analysis (personal); and Activity 2.3, Journal of Ideas—Market Analysis (industry).

2.1 activity "points of pain"

Directions. The purpose of this activity is alert you to the opportunities that occur as the result of unmet needs and gaps in the marketplace. Entrepreneurial opportunities may arise by addressing these "points of pain" for consumers.

Look around you, observe, and talk to others to assess opportunities for improving or developing new products and services or altering existing ones to minimize or eliminate points of pain. Possible things to look for include:

1. The complaints you have or ones you hear from others.
2. Inconveniences you experience when purchasing a product or acquiring a service.
3. A product or service "flaw."
4. Paying way too much for a product or service (i.e. getting "ripped off").
5. A product or service that can contribute to one's health or well-being (literally removing pain of one kind or another).
6. Something that can make life easier.

Over the next 48 hours, list 10 ideas that address "points of pain" you have identified.

	Business (Product/Service) Ideas	Explanation—Points of Pain
1		
2		
3		
4		
5		
6		
7		
8		
9		
10		

Synthesis of "points of pain" activity

Of the 10 ideas noted, which ones appeal to you the most and why?

	Favorite Idea	Why Idea Appeals to Me?
1		
2		
3		

2.2 activity
journal of ideas—marketplace observations and analysis

Directions. Keeping a Journal of Ideas is a process you will want to start now and continue throughout your entrepreneurial career. The table below illustrates the format you might use for such a Journal.

Begin by tuning into your environment, looking closely at the marketplace. What problems are you and others experiencing? What needs or unmet wants do people have? What opportunities are identified in magazines, newspapers, and on the Internet?

	Idea Brief description of idea	**Source of Idea** Solve a problem? Fill a niche? Fill a performance gap? Fulfill a want?	**How Idea Identified** Personal observation? Listening to or talking with others? Newspaper or magazine articles (Include source and date)? Research? Other?
	Example: In-home care for aging parents	Solve a problem	Talking with others, personal experience with parents.
1			
2			
3			
4			
5			
6			

7			
8			
9			

Synthesis of marketplace observations

Of the many ideas noted, which ones appeal to you the most and why?

	Favorite Idea	Why Idea Appeals to Me?
1		
2		
3		

2.3

activity
journal of ideas—industry observations and analysis

Directions. As a framework for answering the following questions, think about the industry in which you currently work or in which you have spent most of your work career. In this activity, you will identify needs, wants, and gaps in that industry that may present entrepreneurial opportunities.

1. Are there products or services that are needed or wanted and are currently unavailable? If so, what are they?

   •

   •

   •

2. Is there a lack of high quality options for certain products or services? If so, what are they?

   •

   •

   •
   I

3. Can you improve upon a product or service that is currently being offered? If so, how would you do so?

   •

   •

   •

4. Is there a market niche with needs that are being overlooked? If so, what niche and needs?

    •

    •

    •

5. Is there a need for more providers of a certain type of product or service? If so, what type of products or services?

    •

    •

    •

Synthesis of industry observation and analysis

Of the many ideas noted in items 1-5 above, which ones appeal to you the most and why?

	Favorite Idea	Why Idea Appeals to Me?
1		
2		
3		

Chapter 7

Catch the Wave—
Identify Trends

In the previous chapter, you learned what made a business idea a winning one, as well as techniques for how to go about identifying a winner. In this chapter, you look at the marketplace to identify trends and anticipate the opportunities they present. But before you get started, let's look at the difference between trends and fads.

A *trend* refers to a general direction or tendency over a period of some duration. A trend provides a substantial "window of opportunity" for entrepreneurs—the time you have to act on an opportunity. *Fads*, on the other hand, are of shorter duration and provide a brief timeframe for acting. Synonyms of "fad" are "craze" and "whim."

The short-term nature of businesses based on fads or one-time events may be viewed as an advantage by some entrepreneurs. They can provide short-term profits without a long-term commitment to running businesses. For example, many businesses have sprung up around the Olympic Games, city, state, and national anniversaries, holidays, or successful local sports teams. The holiday ornament store or Halloween costume shop in the mall are good examples, as are T-shirt vendors promoting your local university's winning sports team. Vendors may literally pop up overnight on every street corner.

Awareness of the short-term nature of these opportunities is the key. Read about one entrepreneur's challenges as a result of depending too heavily on fad merchandise in his store in "Fads Can Be Risky."

Most businesses, however, capitalize on trends, which provide a more solid foundation on which to build a business. They try to catch the wave early, so to speak, and ride it until it crests. But to do so, they have to see it coming.

> **Fads Can Be Risky**
> In Andrew's specialty store, his best-selling product line was a popular, collectible, children's stuffed toy. When customers' interests waned, sales declined. His dependence on this one product group resulted in considerable financial hardship.

Information on trends is readily available in newspapers, magazines, and on the Web. It's as easy as typing www.Entrepreneur.com into your favorite search engine and then entering "trends" in the search box or going to http://trendwatching.com/briefing/. Trade associations are an excellent resource for more specific trend information related to a particular industry.

TIMING AND TRENDS
You've heard the cliché before, "Timing is everything." When it comes to business, it's definitely true.

Many trends have a life cycle, so your timing in entering the market is critical to the success of your business. Identifying a trend early can provide the timeframe you need to develop products and services to capitalize on the trend and enter the market before it becomes crowded with competitors.

If you don't have a business idea, spotting major trends and their related marketplace needs can be a way to identify an idea for a potential business. This was the path followed by Rhianna, whose awareness of the massive aging baby boomer population prompted her to start a business to offer in-home assistance and transportation to allow older adults to live independently in their homes longer. Her business, Angel Connections, provided transportation to and from doctor appointments and shopping trips as well as in-home assistance with customers' non-medical needs.

If you already have a business in mind, identifying supportive trends may provide confirmation that your business idea is a good one. Or you may want to fine-tune your business idea to be more "on-trend," to capitalize upon a trend that is occurring. For example, with almost a third of the aging baby boomer population unmarried, a partnership between AARP and HowAboutWe online dating site has resulted in more than a million users since its inception two years ago.

In her book *Clicking: 17 Trends That Drive Your Business—And Your Life*, Faith Popcorn emphasizes the need for a business to be "on trend" in multiple areas. This is as true today as when Popcorn wrote *Clicking* a number of years ago. Sometimes even minor adaptations to be "on trend" can reap significant results. For example, several national restaurant chains have added healthy, low-calorie menu items to address the growing awareness of our society's obesity problem. Companies that have not adapted, such as Hostess Brands, home of the beloved Twinkie, have suffered the consequences with declining sales and bankruptcy.

Entrepreneurial Clips
* Danielle's technical know-how and marketing background enabled her to start a marketing consulting firm specializing in using social media to promote a product or service.
* Luis started a bookkeeping service for small businesses to capitalize on the growing number of home-based businesses.

INFORMATION ON TRENDS
Information on trends can be found in newspapers and magazines, the Internet, professional journals, and trade associations. *Entrepreneur* and *Business Start-Up* magazines, among others, identify trends in entrepreneurship. For example, on *Entrepreneur Magazine's* Web site (http://www.entrepreneur.com), among the many types of trends listed are technology, social media, and financing.

> *"Prediction is difficult, especially about the future."*
> Yogi Berra

At the time of this writing, a search for books using the keyword "trends" on Amazon.com resulted in a listing of over 74,885 books! A search for "demographic trends" yielded more than 9, 959 titles. A visit to your local library will also provide abundant resources. There is no shortage of information.

Industry associations and their trade shows and conventions are an excellent source of information on the latest industry specific trends. Visiting the Web site www.trendwatching.com is a way to keep abreast of consumer trends. Other helpful

Web sites include www.census.gov, www.pewtrusts.org, www.brookings.edu, and www.jwtintelligence.com, to name a few.

> *"Don't skate to the puck;*
> *skate to where the puck is going to be."*
> Wayne Gretzsky, hockey player

Be a trend spotter in your daily life by observing what's going on in your community and others. Your travels throughout the United States and internationally may alert you to trends that are likely to impact your local area down the road. For example, New York and Los Angeles are known for their fashion forwardness, the West Coast for technology.

Once you have identified an area of interest, determine the market areas which lead the industry in offering cutting edge products or services. For example, certain areas of the country are much further along in environmental conservation than others. These markets provide a glimpse of what is to come in the conservation field.

With so much information available on trends, identifying trend categories can be helpful. Major categories examined in this chapter include technology, demographic, economic, and social.

Demographic Trends

Demographics drive the demand for most consumer products and services, which, in turn, drive the demand for business products. Therefore, the more you know about the demographics of the marketplace, in general, and those to whom you plan to sell, in particular, the better.

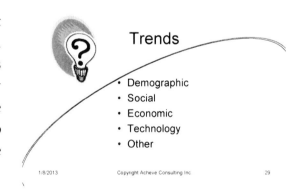

For consumer-based markets, demographic variables include descriptive characteristics such as age, income, gender, education, ethnicity, and occupation. For business-based markets, demographic variables include descriptive characteristics such as number of years in business, number of employees, number of locations, revenue, and industry.

The term "target market" is used to describe the specific group of consumers within the larger market at which a company aims its products and services. The clearer and more specific a company is on the demographic characteristics of its target market, the more effectively it can meet the needs of that market and reach them through advertising and sales activities. See the following table for more specifics about age demographics in the United States.

Note that some of the timeframes listed under "Years" are not mutually exclusive. Also, items listed under "Notable Occurrences" may have been experienced by the generations immediately above or below the generation to which it is attributed. Many of these events took decades to transpire and were experienced by the various generations at different ages—their childhood, youth, or adulthood.

Generations Chart

Century	Generation	Sub-Generation	Years	Notable Occurrences	Population
20th Century	Greatest Generation	G.I. Generation	1901 - 1924	Experienced WWII in adulthood	
		Silent Generation	1925 - 1945	Experienced WWII in childhood, Civil Rights Movement	
	Baby Boomers	Boom Generation / Hippie	1946 - 1964	Space Exploration, First Modern "counterculture"	75 million
	Generation X	Baby Busters	1965 - 1980	Experienced Vietnam War/Cold War	50 million
	Generation Y	MTV Generation / Boomerang Generation	1975 - 1985	Rise of Mass Media/ end of the Cold War	73 million
		Echo Boommers (Sometimes referred to as Millennials)	1978 - 1990	Rise of the Information Age/Internet/War on Terror/Iraq War/Rising Gas and Food Prices	
21st. Century	Generation Z	New Silent Generation	1995 - 2007	Rise of the Information Age/Internet/ dot com bubble Digital Globalization	

Diagram 2.1

- IsaCosta' chart at:
  http://www.esds1.pt/site/images/stories/isacosta/secondary_pages/10%C2%BA_block_1/Generations%20Chart.pdf
- U.S. Census Bureau Chart. *Population by Generation*. 2005. Web. 8 Jul. 2008.

For those of you who anticipate selling to a consumer market, identifying the demographic age group of your targeted customers is an easy way to find out about their general buying habits, lifestyles, mindsets, and needs. Using your favorite search engine, enter the term from the Generation or Sub-Generation columns in Diagram 2.1 that best describes your target market (i.e., Gen X, Baby Boomers). You'll be directed to a wealth of information.

Shifting age demographics and consumer needs influenced by age can be predicted decades in advance. For example, the massive Boomer generation had a significant impact on the need for public schools in the '50s, the housing market in the '70s and '80s, and consumer spending and savings in the last several decades. Many successful businesses resulted from entrepreneurs anticipating the needs and wants of this massive group of buyers. As Boomers age, the impact will be felt in the areas of changing housing needs, health care, and elder services, to name a few. *Hint. Hint. Are there potential business opportunities here?*

Among other significant demographic trends are a greater ethnic diversity in the United States and a lower birth rate since the economic downturn.

Using your favorite Internet search engine, type in "demographic trends" and browse the listing of resources, or google the latest magazine and newspaper articles on trends. Visit the library for additional resources or consult with your local chambers of commerce for demographic trends in your area.

Snapshot of Entrepreneur
Diane James noticed that many of her aging baby boomer friends and acquaintances were having serious concerns about long-term care expenses for their parents as well as for themselves down the road. Some of her friends lacked financial resources to fund nursing home care. Those who had the resources hated seeing their life savings go toward paying nursing home expenses. Diane saw their concerns as a business opportunity.

Her discussions with several financial planners confirmed the need for baby boomers and Gen X'ers to plan for long-term health care for their later years.

By affiliating with a contact she made in her previous job in the insurance industry, Diane established her own agency to sell long-term care insurance to the consumer market. In doing so, she capitalized on both her prior work experience and the demographic trend of the aging population.

Technology Trends

Inventions such as the light bulb, telephone, automobile, computer, and Internet revolutionized the way people lived, communicated and conducted business, leaving in their wake a myriad of products that consumers no longer needed or used. For example, the telephone all but eliminated the telegram; the automobile, the horse and buggy; and the computer and Internet, the use of stationery and greeting cards. Today's products become dated or obsolete at an increasing pace, especially technology-based products.

According to market research firm Gartner, Inc. (cited on eweek.com), technology trends which will significantly impact businesses and organizations in the next few years include tablet computers like Apple's iPad, cloud computing, "big data," and mobile-centric applications and interfaces. Existing technology has matured or become suitable for a wider range of uses while emerging technologies offer strategic business advantages to early adopters. In eWeek it goes on to say that these technologies have the potential for significant market disruption.

Among technology changes on the consumer technology front:
- Slimmer, lighter laptops with longer battery life and more power.
- Smartphones with greater power and functionality, enabling more multitasking.
- New TVs that enable users to browse the web and bring content directly to the device.
- Increased options in the tablet market as other manufacturers introduce alternatives to Apple's iPad. The Microsoft Surface is one such example.

Technology, specifically the Internet and social media, has changed the way businesses advertise and sell their products and how consumers purchase them. This move from bricks and mortar retail stores to online retail sites has created opportunities for small businesses to have a large presence in the virtual world.

"If you are not early, you are late."
John R. Ortego

Economic Trends

The economy has been through some exciting (stressful? disappointing? scary?) times in the last several years. The Dow Jones Industrial Average fell over 700 points on September 28, 2008, and rose over 900 points less than three weeks later, on

October 13, 2008. This excitement continues today as the economic news, both at home and abroad, exerts its sway on consumers, businesses, and financial markets.

The housing market bust, the fall of major financial institutions, and the overhaul of credit markets has significantly impacted both consumers and businesses. Financial institutions have tightened their lending programs. Consumers have altered their spending habits.

It's important to stay abreast of economic news in general and news which directly affects your business and industry in particular. Trade associations are an excellent source of industry-specific information. If you are not aware of an association related to your type of business, google "trade associations xxx," substituting your type of business for "xxx." Adding the name of your city to your search may enable you to identify an organization close to home. Your local yellow pages may also be a resource for identifying local trade associations.

Social Trends

Social trends address changes in lifestyle, values, and culture. Such trends have spawned many new products and services in the marketplace. For example, the trend of more women working outside the home since the '60s supported the growth of child care services, fast food restaurants, and prepackaged foods.

More recent trends include those of more households being headed by older adults, people living alone (marrying later, divorcing, living longer), and a growing health consciousness as obesity hits record highs. These trends have produced an array of marketplace responses such as small-portion food packaging, maintenance-provided communities, and doggie day-care services. Read how Hostess Brands became a business casualty related to the growing need for healthy diets and lifestyles in "No More Twinkies?"

No More Twinkies?
Hostess Brands' beloved Ho Hos, Twinkies, and Ding Dongs may soon be off grocery store shelves. The company's management challenges and failure to meet the needs of a growing health-conscious consumer has resulted in bankruptcy proceedings.

STUDENT WORKBOOK
List trends you have identified and explore the related business opportunities they present in Activity 2.4, Trends, and Activity 2.5, Spotting Trends Before They Reach Your Area.

Similar to trends, which go through stages, products go through stages as well. Their life cycle includes the introduction, growth, maturity, and decline stages. In the following section you explore product life cycle in more depth.

PRODUCT/SERVICE LIFE CYCLE

Understanding product life cycle (PLC) can help you determine which markets present the most potential and when to enter a market. Identifying where your product or service is in its life cycle helps you anticipate opportunities and challenges.

- **Introduction Stage.** When new products are first introduced into the marketplace, they typically require extensive amounts of capital for educating and informing the market. At this stage you are pioneering the way, and pioneering takes time and money. High developmental costs and marketing expenses deter many entrepreneurs from entering at this stage in a product's life cycle. Profitability can be years away.

- **Growth Stage**. Here customers are aware of the product, knowledgeable about it, and ready to buy. The marketplace increasingly demands more, and room exists for additional providers. All-natural and organic baby products, from baby foods to convenience items that make parents days and lifestyles easier, are one example. This stage, with its high demand and profit margins, generally provides the greatest opportunities for new businesses.

    As others spot the business opportunity at this stage, more competition will emerge. One important consideration at the growth stage and the next one, maturity, is whether or not you will be able to set your business apart from others in the market. What will be your competitive advantage?

- **Maturity Stage**. Here demand remains relatively stable or decreases. More and more providers are meeting customers' needs, which often results in aggressive competition and price cutting. Because of numerous large and well established competitors, small businesses often specialize or focus on smaller niche markets to compete. Personal customer service, an advantage that small businesses can have over their larger counterparts, is another key to attracting and keeping customers at this stage.

- **Decline Stage.** This stage is characterized by decreasing product demand and producers leaving the marketplace. In the decline stage, many providers are exiting, not entering, the market. Companies look to innovation as a way to stave off the ravishes of this stage of a products life cycle.

    At this stage you should seriously question entering the market at all. Why would you want to swim against the tide? Why not look for a business that you can catch the wave **before** it crests? In some situations, however, research may reveal that there is still growth potential in a specific trade area, running counter to flat or declining demand in a regional or national market.

Life cycles vary significantly in length of time and the various stages in the life cycle may last weeks or years. Short life cycle products include fashion, some toys (especially ones based on the latest movie releases), and many technology-based products. By comparison, furniture, jewelry, and food products have a much longer life cycle. The shorter the PLC, the shorter the window of opportunity for entrepreneurs to introduce their product or service, build a market, and make sales before demand decreases.

STUDENT WORKBOOK
In Activity 2.6, Product/Service Life Cycle, you identify where your proposed business's main product or service is in its life cycle and explain the rationale for your answer.

2.4 activity trends

Directions. Scan the Internet and various printed sources related to trends, in general, and your area of interest, in particular. List demographic trends in Table A, and technology, economic, and social trends in Table B. Then brainstorm business ideas related to these trends.

Table A

	Demographic Trends	Source of Information	Opportunity Presented (related business ideas)
	Example: Increasing ethnic diversity in the U. S.	*U.S. Census Bureau, 20xx*	*Ethnic magazines and newspapers, grocery stores, restaurants, translation services for employers*
1			
2			
3			
4			
5			

Table B

	Technology, Economic, Social Trends	Source of Information	Opportunity Presented (related business ideas)
	Example: Trend— Young people are waiting longer to marry.	*Star newspaper, January, 20xx*	*Single-serving packaged foods, smaller homes, dog walking services, doggie day care.*
1			
2			
3			
4			
5			

Synthesis of trends

Of the ideas for businesses noted above, which ones appeal to you the most and why?

	Favorite Idea	Why Idea Appeals to Me
1		
2		
3		

2.5 activity
spotting trends before they reach your area

Directions. Choose a product or service category related to your main area of interest. For retail products and services, compare the company listings in that category in your local Yellow Pages with that of another metropolitan area, preferably a larger one some distance away. Yellow Page information for other cities can be obtained over the Internet by accessing www.yellowpages.com. (Note: For business-to-business products and services, you may need to access trade or industry publications to identify companies.)

a. Identify your area of interest.

b. Identify a metropolitan area to use as a comparison.

c. What new or different businesses (products/services) did you find through your comparison?

-
-
-
-
-
-
-

Synthesis of spotting trends early

For products or services identified in item "c" above, which one(s) present a possible business opportunity in your trade area and why?.

	Favorite Idea	Why Idea Appeals to Me?
1		
2		
3		

2.6 activity
product/service life cycle

Directions. Answer the questions below.

a. Based on your knowledge or research of the product/service you plan to offer, at which stage is this product/service in its life cycle—Introduction? Growth? Maturity? Decline? Checkmark your answer below.

___Introduction ___Growth ___ Maturity ___Decline

b. What evidence supports that your product or service is at this stage?

c. What challenges do you anticipate at this stage in your product's/service's life cycle?

d. How will you overcome these challenges?

Chapter 8

Learn from Others

Although many entrepreneurs are looking for the big breakthrough idea, it is often the simple, even mundane one that represents the greatest business opportunity. Rather than coming up with a totally new business idea, sometimes offering an existing product or service efficiently or in an innovative manner will lead to success. Especially when the product or service is experiencing significant sales growth, slight improvements or changes may attract new customers or increase sales to existing ones. By analyzing others businesses and identifying their strengths and weaknesses, entrepreneurs can capitalize on winning ideas in the marketplace.

What has been will be again, what has been done will be done again;
there is no new thing under the sun.

King Solomon

EMULATE

Scan the marketplace to identify successful businesses that you might emulate or replicate. According to research reported by Amar Bhidē in his book *The Origin and Evolution of New Business*, most entrepreneurs start businesses by copying or slightly modifying someone else's idea. He goes on to state that it is not the idea itself but the excellent execution of the idea that differentiates business successes from failures.

Visiting businesses as a consumer and noting what you liked and what you didn't is a great way to ensure that your future customers have the consumer experience you wish them to have. Record your thoughts in a notebook so you will have them when you are ready to start your business. Keep this notebook with you everywhere you go and take advantage of any opportunities you have to visit businesses similar to the one you plan to start. For example, if you will be opening a fitness club, capture the positive and negative aspects of each experience you have visiting others' fitness centers as a way to prepare to open one of your own. If you are opening a retail store, note what you like about the visual layout, décor, and customer service of stores you frequent.

One store manager for a large department store chain commented that her company mandated that she and buyers for the store visit local shops when they were on buying trips, both nationally and internationally, to find "the best thing" that was happening in these stores. Similar efforts to gather market intelligence should be used by small businesses.

CRITIQUE

Critiquing others' businesses and remedying problems you identify is another avenue to business success. It's not just the winners from whom you can learn. From marginal businesses you can observe first-hand how poor merchandizing, marketing, or customer service impacts customers. You can identify products or services that could succeed with a little fine tuning, modification, or better implementation.

It is not uncommon for the inexperienced entrepreneur to dismiss others' businesses and underestimate the loyalty of their customers. Remember, businesses that have been open for a while are meeting consumers' needs at some level or they would not still be in business. Emulating what works and improving upon what doesn't can put your business on the fast track to success.

Entrepreneurial Clips
- Living in Thailand for several years and falling in love with the food was the motivator for Dylan to open the restaurant, Golden Siam, upon his return to the United States. His favorite restaurant in Thailand served as a model for the one he opened in the city in which he grew up.
- Working in a computer service center inspired Cory to start his computer consulting firm to provide the customer service small businesses desired.
- Jun decided to start a shipping service after working in one for two years. From his previous employer, he learned the importance of customer service to improve customer satisfaction and retention.
- Noting the success of a popular coffee shop franchise in which she worked part-time, Hally started her own coffee shop, providing gourmet coffee, bakery items, and Internet access to local patrons.

In Activity 2.7 you will try your hand at applying the technique of modifying others' ideas.

STUDENT WORKBOOK

In Activity 2.7, Making Modifications, you analyze others' businesses to identify what you wish to emulate and what you wish to avoid or change. If your business will be a retail establishment, optional Activity 2.7a, Retail Competitive Analysis Site Visit, is provided to guide your analysis of a retail establishment similar to the one you wish to open.

2.7 activity
making modifications

Directions. In this activity you have the opportunity to look around the marketplace and learn from other businesses as to what works and what doesn't. Make site visits to both successful and not-so-successful businesses; you will learn from both. The more similar the business is to the type you wish to open, the better the learning opportunity.

A. Business Critique

Identify and visit a SUCCESSFUL business that does something extra-ordinarily well (i.e. excellent customer service, unique product). Consider how this business can be replicated, changed, or improved?

Name of Business _____

Address _____

Date of Visit _____

1. Description of products/services offered

2. What is the business doing right?

   •

   •

   •

   •

3. How do the points cited in item "2" apply to the business you are planning?

4. There is always room for improvement, even in successful businesses. How can this business be improved.

    •

    •

    •

5. What other modifications or changes would you suggest?

    •

    •

    •

B. Business Critique
Identify and visit a business that is not a leader in the field and appears to be experiencing some challenges. How can this NOT-SO-SUCCESSFUL business be changed or improved?

Name of Business _____
Address _____
Date of Visit _____

1. Description of products/services offered

2. What is the business doing right? *(Remember, a business that remains open is doing some things right.)*

   •

   •

   •

3. How could this business be improved?

   •

   •

   •

   •

4. What other modifications or changes would you suggest?

-

-

-

-

C. Learning from Others
What have you learned through this activity? Could you replicate or improve upon what is already available in the marketplace? Explain.

2.7a optional activity
retail competitive analysis site visit

(If you are opening a retail establishment, your professor may assign this activity.)
Directions. A detailed analysis of a competitor's retail site and the experience the customer has visiting it provides helpful information for planning your own business.

Name of retail establishment visited _____

Address _____

Date of Visit _____

A. Location:
    ___Shopping center (Checkmark: ___enclosed   ___ strip   ___free-standing)
    ___ Other (specify: _____)

B. Adjacent tenants

C. Other tenants

D. Approximate size of store/office. Circle: "S" "M" "L" or "XL" or estimate square footage_____

E. Visual impression from the exterior:

F. Visual/Atmospheric impression upon entering the store or business (What did it look like? "Feel" like? Smell like?)

G. Sketch store/business layout (i.e. overall shape, primary merchandise areas) Attach separate page of store layout

H. General description of product(s) offered:

I. Merchandise Content Analysis--Detailed description of products offered.

Key Merchandise Classification	# of SKU's:	% of total store stock	Key Vendors	Comments

J. Primary services offered (i.e. major credit cards, return policy, delivery)

K. Best things about this store (What I would emulate?)

L. Worst things about this store (What would I avoid?)

M. Other Observations

Contributed by Donna Duffey, Professor of Entrepreneurship, Johnson County Community College

Chapter 9

Add a Dash of Creativity

In previous chapters, you identified problems, gaps, underserved niche markets, or developing trends in the marketplace. In this chapter you'll learn how to address these opportunities in a creative way, rather than providing the same ho hum product or service to the marketplace. After all, you bring a unique combination of work and life experiences to the table that no one else in the universe has. Here's your chance to shine.

Everyone is creative in some way. When people say they aren't, they are usually thinking of creativity in an artistic sense—visual and performing arts, writing. It's more likely that you exhibit your creativity in the way you live your everyday life. For example, an entrepreneur commented in a small business workshop that he was about as creative as a "rock." Later in his conversation, he went on to discuss his ability to walk into older homes and envision how removing walls and adding windows would update and open the space to appeal to contemporary home buyers. He didn't view this ability as being creative. He felt that anybody could do the same, but he was wrong.

> *"First comes thought;*
> *then organization of that thought into ideas and plans,*
> *then transformation of those plans into reality.*
> *The beginning, as you will observe, is your imagination."*
> Napoleon Hill

Some individuals mistakenly believe they need to invent something new to succeed. With thousands of new products failing each year, reflect on how you can use your creativity to be an *innovator* rather than an inventor. Consider changing and improving something already in the marketplace. Innovation can increase the value proposition for the consumer—what they get in exchange for what they pay. Adding a dash of creativity to a tried-and-true concept may give you the marketplace edge you need.

Regarding innovation, in *Managing for Results,* Peter Drucker suggests that entrepreneurs
- keep it simple, keep it focused.
- start small – try to do one specific thing.

THE CREATIVE PROCESS

There is an air of mystery surrounding the creative process. In his book, *The Art of Thought,* early twentieth-century reformer Graham Wallas summarized his own and others' work on the subject as a four-stage process. Similar versions of his findings are oft repeated in contemporary literature. The stages he identified are Preparation, Incubation, Illumination and Verification. They follow a circular rather than a linear flow, with steps often repeated or circled back to before the process is complete.

Preparation

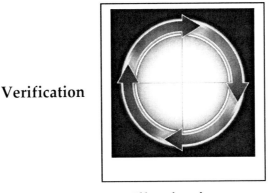

Verification

Incubation

Illumination

Preparation
This stage can be either broadly or narrowly defined. Broadly defined, literally every experience you have ever had prepares you to be creative. In his 2005 commencement address at Stanford, Steven Jobs spoke of how taking a course in calligraphy as a young man at Reed College later influenced the wonderful typography incorporated in Apple's personal computers.

More narrowly defined, preparation includes coursework and/or work experience directly related to an issue. An aspiring entrepreneur enrolling in an entrepreneurship course at the local community college exemplifies this.

As with most things, creativity favors those who are prepared. For example, an artist first learns the basics of color and design; a photographer works with lighting; an entrepreneur studies the marketplace. This preparation lays the foundation for the individual to be able to express his or her creativity within the relevant venues effectively.

Incubation

Just as the name implies, incubation takes time, a scarce resource in today's hurried world. A person needs time for the subconscious mind to combine, integrate, and synthesize often divergent pieces of information in new and different ways. In his book, *The Act of Creation*, Arthur Koestler concludes that processes of discovery, invention, imagination, and creativity share a common pattern which he terms "bisociation." *(Definition of bisociation — the simultaneous mental association of an idea or object with two fields ordinarily not regarded as related [Merriam Webster Online at merriam-webster.com])*

To encourage creative thinking, try this yourself using a forced-choice process of combining a product with an unrelated item or topic. For example, pair a bicycle with various characteristics of a home computer. Pair a restaurant with various characteristics of a ball park. Pair a retail store with various characteristics of a hospital. What combinations occurred? After generating your list of ideas, the next question is, "Do any of these ideas have commercial viability?"

Many everyday items had their origin in this type of bisociation, from wheeled luggage (hand-carried luggage and wagon) to the iPhone (tablet PC and cell phone).

Illumination

The incubation period may take days, weeks, or years. Ultimately a moment of breakthrough occurs when an unconscious thought erupts as a conscious one, that "aha!" moment. This is the point at which you conceptualize or imagine your subconscious thought.

Many times this occurs when a person least expects it—during the middle of the night, driving to work, taking a shower. A relaxed mind allows subconscious ideas to percolate to a conscious level.

Because of the setting in which these "aha!" moments occur, capturing the thought before it slips away may be a challenge. Earlier in this book you learned the value of keeping a Journal of Ideas. Disciplining yourself to record your aha! ideas in your Journal will make them available for future consideration.

Verification

Back to work. Now it's time to determine if your idea has any real value and this requires effort and action on your part. Sometimes termed "implementation," at this point you determine if your idea is "doable." Does your idea work in the real world? Can the product be made? Entrepreneurs determine at this stage if their idea solves a problem, fills a need, or addresses the opportunity presented by a trend. Determining this requires information and research.

"Alternate between imagination and fantasy on one end,
and a rooted sense of reality at the other."
Mihaly Csikzentmihalyi

The Importance of Feedback. Throughout the creative process, it is important to solicit input from others—individuals and groups. During the Preparation Stage, others may provide key pieces of information or unique perspectives. During the Incubation and Illumination Stages, others can be involved in generating new ideas and honing existing ones. Feedback during the Verification Stage is critical to determining the feasibility of an idea. Methods of obtaining feedback include sharing ideas with others, surveying potential customers, or providing the product to the marketplace on a limited basis. For every good idea, many will fall by the wayside.

Blocks to Creativity

As stated earlier, all individuals are creative to some extent. To be creative is to be human. Yet creativity peaks about the time a child enters elementary school. Around that time various factors start coming into play that gradually diminish one's creativity. These include socialization into the education system, as students become more cognizant of the accuracy and appropriateness of their responses, and the increased amount of time children spend interfacing with machines—video games, computers, television—as compared to creative activities.

"Everything that can be invented – has already been invented,"
Charles Duell, Commissioner,
U. S. Patent Office in 1899

Consider the following blocks to creativity by answering the questions in Pause and Reflect that follow.

Pause and Reflect: Blocks to Creativity
Answer the following questions Yes or No.

Do I:
1. Look for the one "right" answer?
2. Fear rejection by others?
3. Fear criticism by others?
4. Fear failure?
5. Avoid ambiguity?
6. Rush to find an answer?

If you answered "Yes" to all or most of these questions, your ability to think creatively will be significantly diminished. All of these items cause you to think "inside the box," so to speak. The first step to overcoming these blocks to creativity is awareness and realizing "there is no box."

The brainstorming activities related to generating business ideas found earlier in the book were designed to overcome several of the blocks to creativity described above. By generating multiple ideas and withholding evaluation of ideas, you are more likely to allow creative thoughts to emerge. Suggestions for increasing one's creativity can be found in books such as *The Seeds of Innovation: Cultivating the Synergy That Fosters New Ideas*, by Elaine Dundon.

"Think Different"
Apple Computer

In the Snapshot of Entrepreneur that follows, read how creativity in solving everyday problems resulted in this entrepreneur's ability to launch new products.

Snapshot of Entrepreneur
When Monte Mitchell had difficulty getting an accurate inside measurement using a traditional tape measure on a home remodeling job, he decided to do something about it. He invented and patented the Measuring Stick, with a built-in level vial, which allows the user to take precise measurements of hard-to-reach areas. His business, Accu-Measure, Inc., sold this unique measuring device through Harbor Freight Tools stores.

Monte started his company with the idea of helping people make their lives easier. He subsequently developed another product as a result of watching a tree-trimming crew cut limbs high above the ground. His product, the Professional Pole Saw, weighs only 5 pounds and has an extension of 22 feet. The Professional Pole Saw is used at numerous golf courses and theme parks around the country.

By being observant about his needs and the needs and frustrations of others, Monte was able to come up with these winning products.

INNOVATION

In the article "The Difference Between Creativity and Innovation," at brainwizard.wordpress.com, author Khan Sajid states, "Creativity is dreaming up a new invention and innovation is making it real in one's own unique way." He goes on to say, "When you bring something new into existence you can say you created it. You cannot say you innovated it. And again when you improve something that already exists, you cannot say you created it but you can say you innovated it."

Khan says that Henry Ford, for example, created the assembly line for car production and the Japanese perfected this concept by introducing their own unique innovations/changes/improvements.

Steve Jobs and Steve Wozniak, who began Apple Computer in 1976, are credited as being the creators of the first personal computer. Continual innovation over the years, however, has resulted in the personal computer as we know it today. Read here how Arm and Hammer continues to innovate, identifying new and different uses for its 165+ year old product, baking soda.

> **Baking Soda Lives On**
> The age-old consumer product Arm and Hammer Baking Soda remains viable today as more and more uses are added, many capitalizing on the "Going Green" trend. How many uses can you name? More than 60 are listed on the Web site: www.green.yourway.net/60-uses-for-arm-hammer-baking-soda-enter-to-win-a-25-visa-gift-card/

Regardless of how you define creativity and innovation, both require preparation, incubation, illumination, and verification.

As with most entrepreneurs, it is likely that your creative talents will be utilized as innovators rather than inventors. Instead of developing a totally new product or service, consider adding a new feature, identifying a new benefit, or reaching a new market for an existing one.

In addition to product/service innovation, you can distinguish your business by being creative in your marketing, packaging, and distribution methods as well. The bisociation method discussed earlier can be used as a technique for doing so. Examine how products or services are marketed, packaged, or distributed in other industries and consider how those techniques can be applied to your products or services.

An example of a jewelry company that did just this is Silpada Designs, which has grown to over a thousand sales representatives in the last 10 years, selling sterling silver jewelry through home parties, a sales technique that has been in the marketplace for decades but was more commonly associated with products such as Tupperware and Pampered Chef kitchen products. Silpada was sold to Avon in 2010 for a reported $650 million (Marketwatch.com).

With services representing a growing percentage of consumer spending, opportunities abound for entrepreneurs to start service business or add, change, or improve upon the service aspects of existing businesses. The former was the case for Abby, whose observation of her employer's difficulty in communicating with his bilingual workforce, coupled with her work experience and bilingual background, led her to start a business specializing in language translation and training for companies that hire large numbers of Hispanic workers. Read "Innovation in Services" for information about new directions in services.

Innovation in Services
A large percentage of business today involves services, estimated to account for 70 percent of the U.S. Gross Domestic Product. A report from Great Britain describes three big changes affecting service industries:
1. The convergence of manufacturing and service innovation where many firms add a "service wrapper" (e.g. post-sales maintenance and support) to the sale of a manufactured product;
2. The growing role of users and consumers in the innovation process; and,
3. Growing concerns about sustainability and the environment.
Source: Department of Business enterprise and Regulatory Reform, United Kingdom. For the complete report, "Supporting Innovation in Services" see www.berr.gov.uk./files/file47440.pdf

Consider how to be innovative in all the key areas related to your business. Using the bisociation process can trigger creativity in these areas.

Product/Service Features. Features describe the physical aspects of the product or service (i.e., a personal computer has a keyboard, monitor, CPU, and software; an accountant's services include data entry, bank reconciliation, and the preparation of financial reports and tax returns).

What additional or new features might benefit your product or service? Examining features of other products or in other industries can jump-start your creative thinking. For example, some restaurants offer online ordering, home delivery, and curbside pick-up. Would these be a desirable feature to add to your planned business?

A word of caution: Features cost money; make sure you are adding ones that customers' value. This is especially true when adding features unrelated to your core business.

Marketing. Study advertising and promotional practices for products and services in different industries to help you identify creative ways to promote your own. For example, what marketing techniques are used by grocery stores? On-line shopping sites? Wholesale clubs? Consulting services? Academic institutions? Airlines? Banks? Will any of their methods work for your business?

Target Markets. Target markets are those customer groups to which you plan to sell. Diagram 2.2 identifies common ways to segment target markets, which are first broken down into either consumer or business markets.

Market Segmentation Variables

Consumer Markets **(Business to Consumer [B to C])**	**Business Markets** **(Business to Business [B to B])**
Geographic factors	Location
Where buyers are located	Number of Employees
Demographic factors	Industry
Age, gender, income, ethnicity,	Sales revenue
occupation, education	
Psychographic factors	
Psychological variables	
Buying motives, personality traits	
Buying patterns	
Frequency, where purchases made	
Lifestyle	
Single, early married, married with children,	
empty nesters, seniors, etc.	

Diagram 2.2

The goal of being able to identify market segmentation variables is to allow you to tailor your products and marketing activities to reach your intended markets. For example, while appealing to a broad range of consumers who are "young at heart," the primary target market for Volkswagen Beetle is Baby Boomer males with higher-than-average incomes, revisiting the nostalgia of their younger years.

Psychographic factors warrant of brief word of explanation. These factors deal with personality, attitudes, intentions, values, interests, lifestyles, and buying patterns and their impact upon buying decisions. There is a great deal of value for a business to know how potential customers live, spend their time and money, and their attitudes and opinions about the world around them

Entrepreneurial Clips
- Nicole changed the target market for her physical therapy practice from two-legged patients to four-legged ones, treating pets instead of people. Additional coursework in canine rehabilitation enabled her to make this transition.
- Leslie targeted corporate clients to expand her catering company beyond her current wedding and private-party markets.

A change in the selection of target markets may create a whole new opportunity, as was the case when office supply companies started focusing on consumer markets instead of business markets. The result was retail giants such as Office Depot and Office Max, which capitalized on the boom of home offices, either for personal or business use. The home remodeling industry experienced similar growth with companies such as Home Depot and Lowes targeting consumers in addition to the building trades. Home Depot's success in the U.S. market did not, however, translate to success in China, where lower labor costs and the high incidence of apartment living resulted in their closing all seven of their remaining stores in the fall of 2012. This was an example of a company failing to grasp the local culture.

Packaging. One form of packaging is the physical box or container that encases a product. Changes in this type of product packaging in the food industry introduced consumers to tuna in plastic pouches, juice in boxes, and cheese in zip-locked bags. When such innovative packaging hit the marketplace, many customers responded "Finally!"

Packaging also refers to combining multiple products in one offering or bundling services together. For example, a custom home builder offered several buyer packages—varying levels of building support. While some customers availed themselves of his full range of services—initial construction planning through home completion—others opted to do some of the work themselves, completing steps like painting and landscaping on their own. In another example, a golf course/club offered various membership packages (family, individual, corporate) including varying amenities (golf, fitness center, restaurant, pool).

Consider how the products or services you plan to sell may be packaged, learning from successful businesses both inside and outside of your industry.

Distribution. Technology has changed the way many products and services are distributed, with the Internet enabling consumers to buy everything from furniture and college textbooks to financial products online. In some cases, customers only take possession of the electronic version of the product, rather than the actual physical product. Electronic books on Kindle or Nook are such examples. Consider how technology can help you distribute your products or services more effectively and efficiently.

For an extensive listing of resources on innovation and creativity, including numerous short videos by leading authorities in the field, go to www.edcorner.stanford.edu. Under "Topics," click on "Creativity and Innovation."

LUCK

There is a bit of serendipity in life, a coming together of circumstances, preparation, and hard work. This is also true in entrepreneurship as well. Many entrepreneurs will tell you that they "got lucky." This comment may reflect humility, but it also reflects reality for a lucky few.

"Luck is what happens when preparation meets opportunity."
Seneca, Roman philosopher

Luck may take the form of overhearing the off-hand comment of a co-worker or reading a certain article in a magazine or newspaper. It might be an astute observation of a marketplace need or gap or a random experience while traveling. It may be the impeccable timing of a product's introduction or initial public offering (IPO). It can be argued that such seemingly random events would remain meaningless without the requisite knowledge and tenacity to turn them into winning opportunities.

"I'm a great believer in luck, and I find the harder I work,
the more I have of it."
Thomas Jefferson

For Dan Dye and Mark Beckloff, the founders of Three-Dog Bakery, now a multimillion dollar global enterprise, this chance happening occurred when a veterinarian told them that one of their three beloved rescue dogs, Gracie, needed the same kind of healthy food, with no preservatives, dyes, or added fats and sugars, that you would feed a sick family member (*The Kansas City Star*). That information, along with the cookie cutter received one Christmas, spawned the original dog "cookies" that were the genesis of their dog bakery business.

You can make your own luck, or at least greatly improve it, by engaging in specific, goal-directed activities, such as those of listening, observing, and researching trends, discussed earlier.

STUDENT WORKBOOK
Complete Activity 2.8, Bisociation, to try your hand at applying a dash of creativity to your business (idea).

2.8 activity
creativity—bisociation

Directions. In this activity, you tap your creative abilities through the bisociation process—putting together things that do not often or naturally occur together. *Note: Your professor may instruct you to complete this activity in small groups. If this is the case, each group member will first share a favorite idea and then the group will select one of the ideas to use for this activity.*

Step 1: Idea

Your Idea	Bisociation Idea
Step 1: Identify your #1 business idea.	**Step 2:** Identify a product/business within a totally different industry.

STEP 2: FEATURES

Your Idea	Bisociation Idea
A. What product/service features do you plan to offer? • • • • • • •	B. What features are common to the product/business you identified for bisociation activity? List them here: • • • • • • •

C. Evaluate. Which, if any, of the features listed under "B" above might be incorporated into your product or service?

Feature to be added	Benefit

STEP 3: TARGET MARKETS

Your Idea	Bisociation Idea
A. For your favorite idea, which markets do you plan to target? List here: ● ● ● ● ●	B. For the product/business identified for the bisociation activity, which markets are being targeted? List them here? ● ● ● ●

C. Evaluate. Could any of the target markets identified in "B" above provide strong potential sales for your business?

Target Market	Why Chosen?

STEP 4: ADVERTISING, PROMOTION, AND SALES

Your Idea	Bisociation Idea
A. How do you plan to advertise, promote, and sell your product/service? List methods here: ● ● ● ● ● ● ●	B. What advertising and promotional methods are common to the product/business you identified for bisociation activity? List them here: ● ● ● ● ●

•	•

C. Evaluate. Could any of the methods you identified in "B" be innovative ways to market your product or service?

Marketing Method	Why Chosen

STEP 5: Packaging

Your Idea	Bisociation Idea
A. How will you "package" your product/service? Describe packaging here. • • • • •	B. How are bisociation products/services packaged? Describe here: • • • • •

C. Evaluate. Could any of the methods identified in "B" be innovative packaging approaches for you product/service?

Packaging Method	Benefits

Chapter 10

Networking

You've heard it said before, "It's who you know that counts." It's true, and it is especially important as you start your own business. Some entrepreneurs will tell you that networking was the skill most critical to their success. Your network may be informal, such as family and friends, or formal, such as trade associations and clubs. Within formal networks, informal ones exist, such as the small group that regularly lunches together after the chamber of commerce meeting. Entrepreneurs access their networks to identify business opportunities, evaluate them for viability, identify resources, and make sales.

Young people starting businesses often have limited networks. Because of this, they must rely heavily on family and friends for early input for their businesses. By the time people reach their 50s and 60s, they typically have extensive networks on which to draw for ideas, information, and support. These networks may include neighbors or professional contacts like your banker or doctor. They may include business colleagues, customers, and suppliers. These contacts may have been made in volunteer situations, such as coaching your child's sports teams, or in professional or social groups—the Rotary Club or golf.

> *"Call it a clan, call it a network, call it a tribe,*
> *call it a family. Whatever you call it,*
> *whoever you are, you need one."*
> Jane Howard, *Families*

By definition, networking involves building supportive systems for sharing information and services among those having a common interest. Often people underestimate the extent of their personal and professional networks. Analyze yours by completing the Pause and Reflect below.

> **Pause and Reflect: Networking**
> Time yourself for two minutes, writing down, on a separate piece of paper, as many names as you can of people that are a part of your personal and professional network. Then count the names on your list and answer the following questions:
> - How many names are on your list?
>
> - How would you describe you network—large and extensive or narrow and focused?
>
> - What are the sources of most of the names on your list?
>
> - Which of the individuals on your list might be helpful in your entrepreneurial endeavors?

NETWORKING AT STARTUP

Many individuals rely heavily on their informal network during the idea and business concept stage of venture creation. For example, they discuss their desire to start a business with family members and close friends and use this network to evaluate the pros and cons of various business ideas.

Since your family and friends know you well, they can help you determine if a business idea fits you, and your skills and interests. They can provide insights that you do not have about your skills and abilities. Friends know a different side of you than family members do, and they have a perspective that may give you additional insights into your strengths.

One caveat, however. If members of your personal network are skeptical of you starting your own business, likely you will not receive the support you need to pursue this goal. If such is the case, broaden your network to include individuals who are more favorably disposed toward entrepreneurship, such as other entrepreneurs or business professionals who provide support to small businesses. This may involve joining organizations that have broad and varied memberships, including entrepreneurs and other business professionals, joining an entrepreneurial networking group, or enrolling in entrepreneurship courses or workshops sponsored by your local college or the Small Business Administration (SBA).

Entrepreneurs will frequently find potential business partners or management team members within their personal and professional networks. Conversely, you may also find that you have skills that would be of value to family members or friends who either have their own businesses or are interested in starting one. You want to be cautious, however, when entering into a business endeavor with family members or friends. Doing so is a business decision and should be treated as such.

The compatibility of partners or team members needs to be evaluated, as well as the extent of common values and goals. Co-authoring the business plan is a good way for potential partners and team members to see if they share a common vision for the business.

Potential advantages of going into business with family and friends include the loyalty of members through difficult times. Stability and the ability to make long-term decisions in a family business can provide a competitive advantage in the marketplace.

Challenges include the carryover of family roles into the workplace and the difficulties this may create. For example, the head of the household may not be the best individual to run the business. Decision making can also be challenging as emotions disrupt the process.

Despite these challenges, family businesses are common. Entrepreneurship tends to run in families. Whether the result of nature or nurture, you may find that you have several relatives who share your interest in entrepreneurship. Clearly defining roles and responsibilities for all positions in the company and treating relationships in a professional, business-like manner can help avoid some of the pitfalls associated with partnering or employing those closest to us.

Snapshot of Entrepreneur
Raised around the small family real estate business, Lonah Birch became actively involved in buying real estate and managing property after the death of her mother. At that time, Lonah developed a business plan and started working her plan. With her husband and partner, she gradually acquired 22 rental units, working up to 20 hours a week, primarily on weekends and in the evening. When the 22 units were paid off, Lonah and her husband felt they could quit their daytime jobs.

Lonah's goal was to provide clean, affordable rental property. She accomplished her goal, averaging a 95 percent occupancy rate, with several residents staying more than a decade.

ONGOING NETWORKING NEEDS

Once you start your business, networking becomes even more important, and you will need an expanded, more formal network. This might include your accountant, attorney, and banker. It may also include entrepreneurs who can mentor you and those who can help you identify and reach potential customers.

Consider including such individuals on an Advisory Committee to ensure continued contact to avail yourself of their expertise. There is much to be learned from more experienced entrepreneurs and seasoned experts.

Advisory Committee members are strategically chosen for the knowledge and experience they can contribute to your business. Such a committee may include an accountant, marketing person, industry specialist, attorney, and other entrepreneurs. The committee typically meets every few months and members share their insights and expertise to assist you in guiding the business. Advisory members are not paid for their time, and meetings are commonly held over breakfast or lunch. As one business's advisory board member commented, "I work for food."

> *"The richest people in the world look for and build networks.*
> *Everyone else looks for work."*
> Robert Kiyosaki

THE NETWORKING PROCESS

Start networking now, even if your business start-up is planned for years down the road. Along the way, you will access your network to find partners, investors, employees, vendors, contract workers, and customers. The first time you talk with someone is typically NOT the time to ask them to buy your product, invest in your business, loan you money, or give you the name of their trusted accountant. Building relationships takes time.

If you don't have the network you need to support your entrepreneurial goals, and many people don't when they are starting out, try a process labeled here as "targeted networking." This term describes the practice of identifying and nurturing relationships with individuals who can contribute to and support your entrepreneurial success.

Targeted Networking

Even though the following process may be intuitive for many people, a closer look at the steps involved can make you become more intentional about it.

Identify an organization. Identify organizations or groups to which potential beneficial contacts belong. This task may be an easy one if you are starting a business related to an industry in which you have worked. If you are venturing into an area new to you, you will need to research potential organizations.

Your research may include asking those in the field for their recommendations as to appropriate organizations, searching the Internet and your local *Yellow Pages* for relevant trade or professional organizations, or checking the *Encyclopedia of Associations* found in most business libraries. Many small business owners also belong to their local chambers of commerce; joining the chamber is an excellent way to connect with other entrepreneurs.

In selecting an organization, determine if its goals are consistent with yours and if it is a vehicle for individuals to exchange information, ideas, support, and contacts. To help with this determination, some organizations will allow you to attend several meetings prior to making a decision to join.

Make acquaintances. The next step is to make acquaintances with people within the organization who can potentially be important members of your entrepreneurial network. To do this, you have to get away from your desk and out of the house and participate in an organization's activities and events.

Make the most of these networking opportunities by arriving early at meetings or staying afterwards to talk with people. Volunteer for activities or hold an office. The more engaged you become, the more easily it will be to get to know others in the group.

Insight or Common Sense
A successful networking relationship includes an emotional connection, reciprocity and advocacy (backing or promoting someone).

Identify win-win opportunities. Effective networking involves identifying people with whom you have something in common and can develop mutually beneficial relationships. Of course, you have to get to know someone before you can identify areas of mutual benefit. Once you do, start building the relationship by offering to help the other person in some manner—sharing a resource, contact's name, or information. And once the relationship has begun, nurture it by maintaining periodic contact—an occasional coffee or lunch does much to keep a relationship alive.

"The currency of real networking is not greed but generosity."

Keith Ferrazzi

Entrepreneurial Clips

- Paul and Kate, a husband and wife team, opened a farm fertilizer, feed, and supply store in their rural community. As farmers themselves, they knew many potential customers, other farmers, in the area.
- Cameron joined the family commercial real estate business and later bought out other family members' shares.
- Brothers Alan and John started a home remodeling business. Alan was the numbers person and John was the craftsman. Together they grew a successful business.
- Randy decided to offer game-bird hunts on his 300-acre farm. As a result of local acquaintances' encouragement after many successful hunts, Randy began advertising these hunts regionally. Participation in hunts grew to the point where he built a separate eating facility to serve hot breakfasts and other meals to the many hunters who visited the farm.
- Megan listened to the encouragement of her colleagues on the arts council of which she was a member and opened an antique and home accessories boutique.
- After repeated requests from family and friends, Wyn increased production of her all-natural, homemade soaps and began marketing them through grocery stores and boutiques.

STUDENT WORKBOOK

Talking to friends and members of your immediate and extended family enables you to identify and clarify your strengths and identify related business ideas in Activity 2.9, Personal Network—Family and Friends. In Activity 2.10, Suggestions from Others, you solicit input from an even broader network of contacts. Your professor may also instruct you to complete Activity 2.10a, Optional In-Class Activity, Suggestions from Others.

Finally, in Activity 2.11, Synthesis of Ideas Generated by Looking Externally, Activities 2.1-2.10, you list all of the ideas you identified in Step 2 in one place.

CONCLUSION TO STEPS 1 AND 2, OPPORTUNITY RECOGNITION

It's time to take stock. You've worked through Step 1, Looking Internally for Business Ideas, and Step 2, Looking Externally for Business Ideas. By now you have a good sense of what an entrepreneurial diamond looks like and what yours are—your strengths and skills. You've also examined the marketplace for possible entrepreneurial diamonds—unmet consumer needs. You solicited business ideas from family, friends, and acquaintances and, along the way, came up with a number of your own.

Throughout you have been encouraged to stay open to new ideas even though you may have started this process with one already in mind. If this was the case, by completing the activities in Steps 1 and 2, you may have changed or refined your idea or gained clarity on its appropriateness for both you and the marketplace.

Now in Activity 2.12, you review all of the potential business ideas you generated in Step 1 and 2 and select the ones you feel most enthusiastic about and which you feel have the greatest potential for success. The work you will complete in Step 3 will help you evaluate the ideas remaining on your list for both personal and market viability.

STUDENT WORKBOOK
Complete Activity 2.12, Synthesis of Steps 1 and 2, in which you review ideas generated and identify the five you believe have the most potential to be rewarding for you personally as well as successful in the marketplace.

STEP 2: INTRODUCTION TO FEATURED ENTREPRENEUR
Delena Stout turned a negative, losing her job, into a positive, starting a successful pet nutrition and bath store. Delena improved her odds of succeeding in this venture by taking a Business Plan course prior to starting her business.

Featured Entrepreneur Delena Stout
Brookside Barkery and Bath

As a displaced worker, Delena Stout had strong reservations about returning to the corporate world, in spite of former jobs with great pay, travel on corporate jets, and work with boards of directors.

During her career, she had worked in accounting, office management, and, most recently, sales and marketing for an architectural firm, but it was through her pets that Delena **came up with her idea** for a business. "We have large dogs. Local places to wash dogs were not clean, had bad equipment, or were inconvenient as large dogs were required to climb up a ladder for a bath," she stated.

By crunching the numbers in a Business Plan course, Delena determined that her business idea—offering self-serve pet baths—would need some fine-tuning to become more profitable. She was able to make the needed adjustments as a result of the information she obtained while **researching the market. "During a trip to the library** in class, I learned how to get on line to pull

up periodicals and newsletters. I delved into layers and layers of research material, and it kept opening doors for me. It was the most fascinating thing I ever did," Delena reported.

"My research on other pet health stores around the country helped me decide to focus on quality," Delena said. Noting that "there wasn't any place in town where we could find good quality pet food," Delena combined pet nutrition with her earlier concept of self-serve baths. Hence her business—Brookside Barkery and Bath—was founded with a

Delena Stout in the middle.

commitment to the health and wellness of pets, stocking the "best quality natural and holistic pet food in the country."

"Through my research," Delena stated, "I learned I was taking a big risk – I was not doing what everyone else was doing. Because I was the first to start this type of business in the area, initial **financing was difficult to obtain**. Finally, a local bank gave me a loan of $25,000; my husband and I took out savings to finance the rest."

Customer response confirmed that there was a need for this type of store and a second location and on-line store have since been opened, with plans to franchise the business in the future, Delena reports.

"Every job I have had in my entire life prepared me for this," Delena said. "Because of my background in marketing, I knew what avenues to use to market the store. My exposure to accounting enabled me to read the business financial statements. Through various work experiences, I also learned what not to do. I would never treat my employees the way I have seen some people treat theirs. I think it is wise to go into business when you are older and have had more life experiences." She advises others that "from the beginning, you **have to have a reason to want to do something. Mine was my animals and their needs**. It's great to see the benefits of good pet nutrition and be able to give back to the community. I couldn't be happier."

For more information, go to www.barkerybath.com

2.9

activity
personal network, family and friends

A. Suggestions from family and friends

Your **family** is a valuable source of entrepreneurial ideas. Talk to three family members and ask for ideas that utilize your strengths, interests, and experiences.

Name	Relationship	Business Ideas Suggested

Your network of **friends** and colleagues see a different side of you than family members do. Talk to three friends/acquaintances and ask them for ideas utilize your strengths, interests, skills, and work experiences.

Name	Relationship	Businesses Suggested

Synthesis of Suggestions from Family and Friends

Perceptions. From your discussion with others and the suggestions they made, what did you learn about their perceptions of your strengths and abilities?

Perceptions of Strengths and Abilities

Ideas. Of the many business ideas made by family members, friends, and acquaintances, which ones appeal to you the most and why? Rank your top three.

Ranking	Idea	Why Idea Appeals to Me
1		
2		
3		

B. Contributing to Others' Businesses

Directions. Identify family members who own their own businesses and brainstorm ways you can contribute to these businesses. Withhold evaluation of the feasibility or desirability of doing so at this time.

Name	Relationship	Type of Business	How You Can Contribute

C. Entrepreneurial Support System

Directions. From your circle of family, friends, and acquaintances, which individuals might become a part of your personal support network or a resource for you in starting your own business?

Name	Relationship	How He/She Might Be Helpful or Supportive

2.10 activity suggestions from others

Directions. In addition to the family members and friends you consulted with in activity 2.9, interview three acquaintances(i.e. neighbors, professors, co-workers, classmates) to generate business ideas. Use the Interview Guides that follows to interview those listed.

	Name	Source of Relationship
1		
2		
3		

Interview Guide #1

Name of Contact _____ Date _____

1. What needs have you observed in the marketplace?

2. What types of products or services would you like to see offered in more variety? Of higher quality? At a more reasonable price? Packaged differently?

3. What problems have you experienced in meeting your personal needs in the marketplace? Business needs?

4. If **you** were to start a business today, what type of business would you start and why?

Interview Guide #2

Name of Contact _____ Date _____

1. What needs have you observed in the marketplace?

2. What types of products or services would you like to see offered in more variety? Of higher quality? At a more reasonable price? Packaged differently?

3. What problems have you experienced in meeting your personal needs in the marketplace? Business needs?

4. If **you** were to start a business today, what type of business would you start and why?

Interview Guide #3

Name of Contact _____ Date _____

1. What needs have you observed in the marketplace?

2. What types of products or services would you like to see offered in more variety? Of higher quality? At a more reasonable price? Packaged differently?

3. What problems have you experienced in meeting your personal needs in the marketplace? Business needs?

4. If **you** were to start a business today, what type of business would you start and why?

© Achēve Consulting Inc.

Synthesis of suggestions from others

Of the ideas contributed by others, which ones appeal to you the most and why?

	Favorite Idea	Why Idea Appeals to Me
1		
2		
3		

2.10a optional in-class activity suggestions from others

Directions. Your professor may instruct you to complete this activity in a small group. To do so, form groups of 4-6 students. List students' names here:

_____   _____
_____   _____
_____   _____

Record group members' individual responses in the Synthesis section of activity 2.10.

Student Name	Ideas in Synthesis Section of Activity 2.10

From the ideas each person individually listed in activity 2.10, identify the 3 your group feels are most likely to be successful. Explain why.

	Idea	Why Group Feels Idea Will Be Successful
1		
2		
3		

Contributed by Donna Duffey, Professor of Entrepreneurship, Johnson County Community College

2.11 activity
step 2—synthesis, ideas generated by looking externally, activities 2.1- 2.10

Directions

Activities that included a "Synthesis" section are identified in Column 1. Refer back to these activities and list the ideas included there in Column 2 below.

Activity	Synthesis List of Ideas
2.1	
2.2	
2.3	
2.4	
2.5	
2.9	
2.10	

Synthesis of ideas generated in Step 2

Of the ideas listed above, which five appeal to you the most and why?

	Favorite Idea	Why Idea Appeals to Me
1		
2		
3		
4		
5		

2.12 activity
synthesis of steps 1 and 2, looking internally and externally for business ideas

Directions. Review Step 1 Synthesis in activity 1.5 **and** Step 2 Synthesis in activity 2.11. Record below the five ideas:

- About which you are most enthusiastic.
- Which you feel have the greatest potential.
- Which are most closely related to your work experience, education, skills, and talents.

	Idea	Why Selected (Explain your choice.)
1		
2		
3		
4		
5		

Step 3

Screening Business Ideas

Step 3 Objective

To screen ideas on the basis of how they
- Fit your talents and skills.
- Meet your personal and professional goals.
- Meet your financial goals.
- Address marketplace needs.

Chapter 11

Evaluating Ideas: Talents and Skills

In Steps 1 and 2, you looked at yourself and the marketplace for potential business ideas. In doing so, you identified many. Now comes the challenge of evaluating these ideas to identify the one you would like to pursue.

A business idea is right for you if it is one for which you have the talents and skills to launch and grow. It is one that fulfills your personal and professional goals. It is an idea for which the financial and emotional rewards outweigh the risks you assume as a business owner and for which you have the funds to launch. Finally, it is one that fulfills a marketplace need.

The Screening Process

- Skills and Talents
- Dreams and Goals
- Personal Finances
- Market Viability

1/8/2013   Copyright Acheve Consulting Inc   32

In this chapter, you'll start the screening process by assessing your skills, talents, and entrepreneurial characteristics and evaluate your qualifications for the businesses you are considering.

All people possess characteristics that make them special or different, and define their place within the family, peer group, school, or work environment. What do you do well? At what have others told you that you excel? What have you received recognition for in the past. These talents and skills may be the source of **your** competitive advantage. This was the case with Isabella, an interior designer whose talents as an artist allowed her to provide sketches and renderings of decorating projects with quality unmatched by her colleagues. Earlier in the course, you reflected upon the skills and talents you possess by analyzing work experiences, hobbies, and academic and early successes.

Having a skill, talent, or interest around which to build a business is just one part of a recipe for business success. Another part is having the entrepreneurial expertise to launch, manage, and grow a business. The latter may be the part you are unsure of. This uncertainty is what keeps many aspiring entrepreneurs from following their dreams.

Entrepreneurship used to be a closed society. A person learned it around the dinner table, and, if you didn't have the right people sitting at the table, you weren't sure how it worked. Luckily, colleges and even high schools today teach students entrepreneurial basics and processes. There is also more public awareness and support for entrepreneurs than there used to be.

But even with the growing awareness of the importance of entrepreneurship to our economy, there is still some mystique surrounding it. Stories about today's entrepreneurial cult heroes only enhance the mystique. How can one compare to entrepreneurs like Bill Gates, Steve Jobs, and Michael Dell?

The list of impressive "entrepreneurial characteristics" included in many books can also be intimidating, making it appear that you need extraordinary talents and skills to succeed in business. Not so. Look around you. You likely know a number of successful entrepreneurs—the owner of your favorite restaurant, the dental office you visit, or the auto supply store on a nearby corner. These entrepreneurs are all similar to you.

WHAT IT TAKES

Let's start out by emphasizing that there is no single list of requisite entrepreneurial characteristics for success. However, certain commonalities occur. They are likely to include

- Sensitivity to and awareness of opportunities in the marketplace
- Persuasiveness and ability to network with others
- Determination and passion
- Ability to market a good or service

It is helpful to start out with a realistic idea of the skills, attributes, and temperaments that assist entrepreneurs in launching and growing a business. Then determine which ones you possess. For those you don't, determine how much of a barrier they present and if a strategy can be developed to acquire the missing ones.

In this book, the term "skills" is used to describe abilities or proficiencies that have a strong learning component. Even though some innate aptitudes may be involved, skills typically involve coursework, training, or work experience. For example, financial expertise is a skill. You may have an analytical mind and be good with numbers, but you still need to take financial/accounting courses or learn finance and accounting on the job to understand financial statements.

With skills, sometimes you can get by with having a basic understanding in the area and then relying on partners, employees, contract workers, or consultants to shore up your lack of in-depth expertise.

Attributes and temperaments (traits), collectively termed "characteristics," are typically viewed as more innate. You likely need to possess these characteristics yourself rather than look to others to shore up your deficiencies. For example characteristics, such as perseverance and determination, are critical to entrepreneurial success. See the "Entrepreneurial Attitudes" textbox for more information on this subject.

In the following sections you will determine to what degree you possess important entrepreneurial characteristics and skills, and how to address those which need strengthening.

Entrepreneurial Attitudes
How do entrepreneurs think about themselves? The recent study "Entrepreneurial Attitudes and Action in New Venture Development" offers some insights. The study found that positive attitudes (e.g., sense of self-efficacy, confidence and commitment) enable entrepreneurs to persist amid the uncertainty and instability of the start-up process. Another interesting finding is that there seems to be a direct association between entrepreneurial attitudes and venture performance, although this finding is not as strong.

Entrepreneurial Attitudes and Action in New Venture Development by Rose Trevelyan, Australian School of Business, University of South Wales, as reported by the Ewing Marion Kauffman Foundation at www. entrepreneurship.org

Entrepreneurial Characteristics

Entrepreneurial characteristics, or "traits" as they are frequently called, include a broad array of attributes and temperaments, such as creativity, self-confidence, and perseverance. A common criticism of the trait approach for analyzing entrepreneurial success is that these traits are not unique to entrepreneurs but describe many leaders and managers as well.

The study "Entrepreneurial Behavior" by Sharda Nandram and Karel Samsom overcame many of the drawbacks of the trait approach by also looking at entrepreneurial actions or behaviors.[1] It described what successful entrepreneurs *do* in addition to what they *are*, and it recognized the interplay of the individual with his or her environment.

Nandram and Samsom's findings indicate that to be successful, an entrepreneur must
1. be watchful to spot the opportunities needed to start an entrepreneurial activity,
2. be persuasive in seeking cooperation or investment,
3. take time for reflection (a unique finding in terms of prior research) in order to learn from own experiences,
4. be goal oriented in order to work efficiently,
5. be decisive,
6. be pragmatic to decrease the uncertainty and flexibility in the environment and
7. finally, have self confidence in order to face success but also failures.

Nandram and Samsom go on to say that needed **attributes** for entrepreneurs are (1) creativity, (2) courage, (3) trustworthiness and (4) ambition. They identified **temperaments** needed as (1) capacity for empathy, (2) resoluteness, (3) perseverance, (4) internal locus of control*, and (5) determination. *Internal locus of control refers to a person's perception that he or she is responsible for what happens in his or her life.*

Although not listed in the Nandram and Samson study, another attribute commonly attributed to entrepreneurs is risk taking. While some think of entrepreneurs as high

---

[1] *Nandram, Sharda, and Karel J. Samsom. *New Perspectives Gained through the Critical Incident Technique.* Nyenrode Business Universiteit, Apr. 2007. Web. 5 Jan. 2009. NRG Working Paper Ser. 07-04.

risk takers, research shows they tend to be calculated risk takers, that they undertake risks after careful assessment of potential outcomes.

> *"Often the difference between a successful man and a failure is not one's better abilities*
> *or ideas but the courage that one has to bet on his ideas,*
> *to take a calculated risk—and act."*
>
> Maxwell Maltz

In Activity 3.1, you evaluate yourself on risk taking and the characteristics and behaviors included in the Nandram and Samson study. Then, recognizing that self-perception is not always accurate, you'll ask others to assess you as well.

If you find allot of consistency among others' evaluations, a clear picture of your skills and strengths will emerge. If evaluations vary a great deal, you will want to ask additional friends and family members to complete assessments. This additional input, together with your initial evaluations, may uncover your strengths and weaknesses.

Once you do have a clear picture, what do you do with this information? This data can be helpful if you are questioning whether or not starting a business is right for you. It can also help you determine when to bring others into your decision-making process, when to hire others to perform certain types of work, or what to look for in potential management team members.

> *"Many of life's failures are people*
> *who did not realize how close they were to success*
> *when they gave up."*
>
> Thomas A. Edison

If you are interested in obtaining additional information about your personal characteristics and attributes and how they compare to others in various careers, contact the counseling or career center at your local college or university and inquire about assessment tools such as the Myers-Briggs Type Indicator® (MBTI) personality inventory, DISC Personality Profile or similar instruments. Some of these assessment tools are also available online.

Entrepreneurial Skills

In addition to the entrepreneurial attributes and characteristics identified in the previous section, certain skills are needed for entrepreneurs to launch and run their businesses. Many books, articles, and Web sites identify these "must-have" skills, and no two lists are alike. However, there are some commonalities:

- Financial forecasting, analysis, and cash flow management
- Marketing and sales—market analysis, advertising, promotion, selling, and networking
- Management—planning, leadership, communications, and problem solving
- Technical expertise—computers, data processing, spreadsheet, Internet
- Operations—production, quality control, and administration

For many entrepreneurs, here is where the challenges begin. Whether because of lack of knowledge or lack of interest, the tendency to neglect key management areas has doomed more than one entrepreneurial business. Awareness of their importance is the first step to remedying this problem. This challenge is aptly described by entrepreneur Dave Polney below.

"The easiest thing to do is to work IN your business.
It's much harder to manage your business.
The work is second nature to you; management isn't."
Dave Polney, owner, 190 SL Services

In Activity 3.1 you'll identify your entrepreneurial strengths and consider how the business ideas you have will utilize them.

STUDENT WORKBOOK
Go to Activity 3.1a - c, Personal Assessment and Matching Ideas with Strengths, and first complete the assessment yourself, then disseminate it to others. Then in Activity 3.1d, evaluate the business ideas you have against the strengths you identified through these assessments.

STRENGTHENING WEAKNESSES
After completing Activity 3.1, you will have a clearer idea of what strengths you bring to a business. This awareness enables you to identify the skills and abilities you need to nurture and grow. Following are ways you can jump-start your learning curve to acquire or sharpen skills more rapidly.

Work in the Field
Time you can devote to working in the field in which you plan to start a business will reap tremendous benefits. A minimum of two to three years experience is preferable.

If you can't afford to quit your job to work full-time in the field in which you wish to start a business, consider working part time in it. Any job within the new field can provide a learning experience, even one you feel is beneath your skill level.

Find a Mentor

Identifying a mentor is an important next step on your entrepreneurial journey; most successful entrepreneurs report having one. Some identify a series of mentors who guided them along the way, as their mentoring needs changed with the growth of their businesses.

Mentors are likely to be other entrepreneurs or professionals who know the ropes of launching and growing a business. They may be friends or former colleagues who have started their own businesses. Mentoring relationships may grow out of friendships developed through clubs, industry associations, or volunteer activities. Like other relationships, they grow slowly and take time and energy on the part of both parties.

> *"If you want to go somewhere, it is best*
> *to find someone who has already been there."*
> Robert Kiyosaki

Your community may have an entrepreneurial mentoring program. These are typically started by successful local entrepreneurs as a way of "giving back" to their communities. Free online mentoring is also available through SCORE. Their Web site address is score.org/ask_score.html.

Insight or Common Sense
It's hard to know what you don't know. Nurture relationships with those who are more knowledgeable and experienced in the field and who can guide you during the early and growth stages of your business.

Yet another source of mentoring may be a "competitor at a distance." This is someone with a business like yours but outside your trade area. As long as your business does not compete with theirs, such a person may be very willing to share information and hard-learned lessons.

Competitors at a distance can be located through the *Yellow Pages* from other communities, the Internet, your trade association, or by talking with people in the industry. Although an introduction through a third party is an even better way to make the acquaintance of such a person, entrepreneurs report success using a "cold call" approach as well.

To be successful, mentoring relationships need to be win-win. The reward for the mentor is often the feeling of satisfaction that comes from "giving back," helping others.

Personal coaches may fulfill mentoring roles for some entrepreneurs, as was the case with entrepreneur Kathy Yeager, featured here.

Snapshot of Entrepreneur
After working 30 years in Workforce Development and Continuing Education at Johnson County Community College, Kathy Yeager decided it was time to retire. She started planning her retirement a year in advance, recognizing that other colleges would benefit from her sales and marketing expertise and experience. That's when Kathy contracted with a personal coach, who worked with her for an hour a month on such things as identifying her products and targeting her market. "My coach helped me stay focused on the next steps to start and develop the business. She really helped me find the right resources, focus on my core business and set goals," Kathy said. In addition, Kathy sought the services of the Small Business Development Center at her college where she received guidance on business concept development and the preparation of her business plan. By the time Kathy retired, her consulting business was off to a strong start, with clients from across the country.

Contract Training Edge, LLC, Kathy's consulting business, is a resource for colleges nationwide in the area of solution selling, workforce development, benchmarking, reorganization and restructuring, and one-on-one coaching. For more information, contact Kathy Yeager kyeager@ctedge.net, or www.ctedge.net.

Volunteer Your Services
A carefully selected volunteer situation in the right setting may allow you to learn the business and industry in which you will eventually open your business. As a volunteer, you have the opportunity to contribute and at the same time learn new skills. While you are learning, you are also expanding your network of people who may be helpful to you down the road. And it's hard for others to turn down

Volunteering Leads to Partnership
With an eye toward a possible partnership, Elaina volunteered time working at a local gift boutique for over a year prior to formalizing a partnership arrangement with the owner.
This gave both parties the opportunity to work together and test their compatibility prior to making a commitment to the relationship. Elaina likened the experience to dating prior to getting married.

"free" labor. Unpaid positions are not strictly for 20-year-old student interns.

Read "Volunteering Leads to Partnership" for an example of how a volunteer situation proved beneficial to both parties involved.

Develop New Skills

The less experience you have in the field, the steeper the learning curve. Plus running a business, especially if it's your first, has its own learning curve. So hang on, you're in for an exciting adventure!

In addition to the technical knowledge of your business—what you will do in your business—you need sales and marketing know-how, financial acumen, operations expertise, and knowledge of legal issues impacting your business. The good news is that you don't have to do everything yourself.

Contrary to popular folklore, entrepreneurship is not a lone-wolf experience. Successful entrepreneurs put together teams which complement their strengths and shore up their weaknesses. So even though early on you'll likely have to be a jack-of-all-trades and perform many of these functions yourself, as your business grows you will be able to expand your team to include others who have the necessary skills. In areas such as taxes and employment law, you'll need expert advice from the beginning.

"Entrepreneurship is a team sport."

Even if you don't need to acquire a skill yourself, you will need to be able to communicate with those who provide that skill to your business. For example, you will interact with your accountant and attorney and need to understand the information they provide to effectively manage your business.

Talking to entrepreneurs and others in the field is an excellent way to identify individuals who have the talents you need. Contact your local Small Business Development Center or Small Business Administration office for help in identifying resources as well. The SBDC is a cooperative effort of the private sector, the educational community and federal, state, and local governments, and provides assistance to current and prospective small business owners. SCORE, a nonprofit association which bills itself as "Counselors to America's Small Business," is a partner with the U.S. Small Business Administration. Their goal is to educate entrepreneurs in starting and growing small businesses nationwide. Both offer free services to entrepreneurs and can be found through their Web sites:

SBA: http://www.sba.gov/localresources

SBDC: http://www.sba.gov/aboutsba/sbaprograms/sbdc/index.html

A heads up. You will be heavily involved in the sales and marketing of your products/services, especially early in the business. It falls to you to test market demand and grow your business to the point where you may be able to hire others to assist with these functions. If you are not knowledgeable about sales and marketing, consider enrolling in sales or marketing courses through your local college or sign up for short "how-to" courses offered through your local SBA or SBDC. Talking to entrepreneurs who sell similar products or marketing consultants is also helpful.

Even with knowledge, however, some entrepreneurs don't have the temperament for sales. If such is the case and you feel this challenge cannot be overcome, consider hiring or contracting with sales talent from the start.

Today, more so than in the past, a business may be supported by a virtual workforce with team members and employees from around the country or world, e-mailing work and meeting via telephone conference calls, Webinars, and virtual meetings.

Entrepreneurial Clips

- Angela's financial and marketing expertise and entrepreneurial experience led her to seek out businesses that were in trouble and which she could acquire, turn around, and sell.
- Nick gradually acquired multiple small apartment buildings, which he managed himself. His strong sense of independence, financial acumen for buying properties when the price was right, and skills in repair work contributed to his business success.

In Activity 3.2, you decide where your talents can be aptly used in your business, what skills you need to further develop, and when to look to others for needed attributes and skills.

STUDENT WORKBOOK

Complete Activity 3.2, Addressing Gaps, in which you identify ways the information acquired through your personal and peer evaluations in the previous activity will help you as you plan your business.

3.1

activity
personal assessment and
matching ideas with strengths

Directions. Complete forms as instructed to do.

3.1a. Personal Assessment
Assess your talents, skills, and characteristics by rating yourself on the inventory provided in activity 3.1a. Prior to doing so, review activities 1.1, 1.2, and 1.3 completed earlier in the course, which highlight your talents and skills.

3.1b. Peer Assessment
Ask three or more friends or family members to assess your skills and characteristics by completing the inventory in 3.1b. Three copies of the inventory are included here. They are printed front side only to facilitate their distribution to different parties. If additional copies are needed, you may photocopy activity 3.1b to expand this activity.

3.1c. Composite Inventory, Strengths and Weaknesses
Combine Peer Assessments on the form provided in activity 3.1c. Then identify your strengths and areas for further development.

3.1d. Matching Strengths and Business Ideas
Referring back to your Composite Inventory (activity 3.1c) review the business ideas listed in activity 2.12, Synthesis of Steps 1 and 2, to identify the ideas that best utilize your strengths.

3.1a personal assessment

Directions. Assess your own talents, skills, and characteristics. Prior to doing so, review activities 1.1, 1.2, and 1.3, which highlight your talents and skills.

A. **Identify Talents and Strengths.** Reflect on strengths/competencies at which you excel and identify them here.

B. **Assess Strength of Attributes, Behaviors, and Entrepreneurial Skills.** For each numbered item listed below, indicate the **degree** to which the attribute/temperament/behavior is possessed or exhibited by writing a 1, 2, 3, 4, or 5 on the line in front of each number.

Scale: 1–absent   2–low   3–moderate   4–slightly high   5–very high

Attributes and Temperaments

___ 1. Creativity
___ 2. Courage
___ 3. Trustworthiness
___ 4 Ambition (high achievement orientation)
___ 5. Capacity for empathy

___ 6. Resoluteness
___ 7. Perseverance
___ 8. Internal locus of control (feeling you control your own destiny)
___ 9. Determination
___ 10. Calculated risk taker

Behaviors

___ 11. Watchful to spot the opportunities needed to start an entrepreneurial activity
___ 12. Persuasive in seeking cooperation or investment
___ 13. Takes time for reflection in order to learn from own experiences
___ 14. Goal oriented, in order to work efficiently
___ 15. Decisive
___ 16. Pragmatic, to decrease the uncertainty and flexibility in the environment
___ 17. Self-confident, in order to face success and failures

Entrepreneurial Skills

___ 18. Financial—forecasting, analysis, cash flow management
___ 19. Marketing and sales—market research and analysis, advertising, promotion, selling, networking
___ 20. Management—planning, leadership, communications, problem solving
___ 21. Technical expertise—data processing, spreadsheets, Internet
___ 22. Operations—production, quality control, administration

C. **Identify strengths.** List the 5 attributes, behaviors, or skills on which you rated yourself the highest in section "B."

3.1b peer assessment #1

Directions. Complete the following.

A. Identify Talents and Strengths. Reflect on strengths/competencies at which the individual excels and identify them here.

B. Assess Strength of Attributes, Behaviors, and Entrepreneurial Skills. For each numbered item listed below, indicate the **degree** to which the attribute/temperament/behavior is possessed or exhibited by writing a 1, 2, 3, 4, or 5 on the line in front of each number.

x————————x————————x————————x————————x

Scale: 1–absent 2–low 3–moderate 4–slightly high 5–very high

Attributes and Temperaments

___ 1. Creativity
___ 2. Courage
___ 3. Trustworthiness
___ 4 Ambition (high achievement orientation)
___ 5. Capacity for empathy

___ 6. Resoluteness
___ 7. Perseverance
___ 8. Internal locus of control (feeling you control your own destiny)
___ 9. Determination
___ 10. Calculated risk taker

Behaviors

___ 11. Watchful to spot the opportunities needed to start an entrepreneurial activity
___ 12. Persuasive in seeking cooperation or investment
___ 13. Takes time for reflection in order to learn from own experiences
___ 14. Goal oriented, in order to work efficiently
___ 15. Decisive
___ 16. Pragmatic, to decrease the uncertainty and flexibility in the environment
___ 17. Self-confident, in order to face success and failures

Entrepreneurial Skills

___ 18. Financial— forecasting, analysis, cash flow management
___ 19. Marketing and sales—market research and analysis, advertising, promotion, selling, networking
___ 20. Management—planning, leadership, communications, problem solving
___ 21. Technical expertise—data processing, spreadsheets, Internet
___ 22. Operations—production, quality control, administration

C. Identify strengths. List the 5 attributes, behaviors, or skills on which individual rated the highest in section "B."

3.1b peer assessment #2

Directions. Complete the following:

A. Identify Talents and Strengths. Reflect on strengths/competencies at which the individual excels and identify them here.

B. Assess Strength of Attributes, Behaviors, and Entrepreneurial Skills. For each numbered item listed below, indicate the **degree** to which the attribute/temperament/behavior is possessed or exhibited by writing a 1, 2, 3, 4, or 5 on the line in front of each number.

x————————x————————x————————x————————x

Scale: 1–absent   2–low   3–moderate   4–slightly high   5–very high

Attributes and Temperaments

___ 1. Creativity
___ 2. Courage
___ 3. Trustworthiness
___ 4 Ambition (high achievement orientation)
___ 5. Capacity for empathy

___ 6. Resoluteness
___ 7. Perseverance
___ 8. Internal locus of control (feeling you control your own destiny)
___ 9. Determination
___ 10. Calculated risk taker

Behaviors

___ 11. Watchful to spot the opportunities needed to start an entrepreneurial activity
___ 12. Persuasive in seeking cooperation or investment
___ 13. Takes time for reflection in order to learn from own experiences
___ 14. Goal oriented, in order to work efficiently
___ 15. Decisive
___ 16. Pragmatic, to decrease the uncertainty and flexibility in the environment
___ 17. Self-confident, in order to face success and failures

Entrepreneurial Skills

___ 18. Financial—forecasting, analysis, cash flow management
___ 19. Marketing and sales—market research and analysis, advertising, promotion, selling, networking
___ 20. Management—planning, leadership, communications, problem solving
___ 21. Technical expertise—data processing, spreadsheets, Internet
___ 22. Operations—production, quality control and administration

C. Identify strengths. List the 5 attributes, behaviors, or skills on which you rated the individual the highest in section "B."

3.1b peer assessment #3

Directions. Complete the following:

A. Identify Talents and Strengths. Reflect on strengths/competencies at which the individual excels and identify them here.

B. Assess Strength of Attributes, Behaviors, and Entrepreneurial Skills. For each numbered item listed below, indicate the **degree** to which the attribute/ temperament/behavior is possessed or exhibited by writing a 1, 2, 3, 4, or 5 on the line in front of each number.

x————————x————————x————————x————————x

Scale: 1–absent   2–low   3–moderate   4–slightly high   5–very high

Attributes and Temperaments

___ 1. Creativity

___ 2. Courage

___ 3. Trustworthiness

___ 4 Ambition (high achievement orientation)

___ 5. Capacity for empathy

___ 6. Resoluteness

___ 7. Perseverance

___ 8. Internal locus of control (feeling you control your own destiny)

___ 9. Determination

___10. Calculated risk taker

Behaviors

___ 11. Watchful to spot the opportunities needed to start an entrepreneurial activity

___ 12. Persuasive in seeking cooperation or investment

___ 13. Takes time for reflection in order to learn from own experiences

___ 14. Goal oriented, in order to work efficiently

___ 15. Decisive

___ 16. Pragmatic, to decrease the uncertainty and flexibility in the environment

___ 17. Self-confident, in order to face success and failures

Entrepreneurial Skills

___ 18. Financial—forecasting, analysis, cash flow management

___ 19. Marketing and sales—market research and analysis, advertising, promotion, selling, networking

___ 20. Management—planning, leadership, communications, problem solving

___ 21. Technical expertise—data processing, spreadsheets, Internet

___ 22. Operations—production, quality control, administration

C. Identify strengths. List the 5 attributes, behaviors, or skills on which you rated the individual the highest in section "B."

3.1c

composite
strengths, attributes, behaviors, and entrepreneurial skills

A. Synthesis of Composite Talents and Strengths
Directions. Record talents or strengths identified by multiple survey respondents in item "A" of peer assessments (3.1b).

B1. Composite Attributes and Temperaments
Directions. Copy the scores from peer assessments to Column 1. Then calculate the averages of these scores and record them in Columns 2. Do <u>not</u> include personal assessment scores (activity 3.1a) in calculations.   Repeat process for each item listed.

Col. 1	Col. 2	Col. 3		Col. 1	Col. 2	Col. 3
Record Peer Scores	Calculate Average Score	Attributes and Temperaments		Record Peer Scores	Calculate Average Score	Attributes and Temperaments
		1. Creativity				6.Resolute-ness
		2.Courage				7.Persever-ance
		3.Trustworth-iness				8.Internal locus of control (feeling you control your own destiny)
		4. Ambition high achieve-ment orientation				9. Determina-tion
		5.Capacity for empathy				10.Calculated risk taker

B2. Composite Behaviors

Column 1	Column 2	Column 3
Record Peer Scores	Calculate Average Score	Behaviors
		11. Watchful to spot the opportunities needed to start an entrepreneurial activity
		12. Persuasive in seeking cooperation or investment
		13. Takes time for reflection in order to learn from own experiences
		14. Goal oriented, in order to work efficiently
		15. Decisive
		16. Pragmatic, to decrease the uncertainty and flexibility in the environment
		17. Self-confident, in order to face success and failures

B3. Composite Entrepreneurial Skills

Column 1	Column 2	Column 3
Record Peer Scores	Calculate Average Score	Entrepreneurial Skills
		18. Financial—forecasting, analysis, cash flow management
		19. Marketing and sales—market research and analysis, advertising, promotion, selling, networking
		20. Management—planning, leadership, communications, problem solving
		21. Technical expertise—data processing, spreadsheets, Internet
		22. Operations—production, quality control and administration

B.4 Synthesis of Composite Attributes, Temperaments, Behaviors, and Skills

Directions: For all sections of item "B" (B1-B3) review average scores (Column 2) and identify your highest averages, your strengths. List strengths below.

3.1d activity, matching strengths and business ideas

Directions. Reflecting on the strengths identified on the Composite Inventory (3.1c) which business ideas listed in activity 2.12 best utilize your skills, talents, and abilities? Identify 3 ideas below.

	Idea	Explanation of Idea
1		
2		
3		

3.2 activity addressing gaps

Directions. Based on the information obtained through the personal and peer assessments completed in activity 3.1, do the following:

A. Compare your personal assessment, activity 3.1a, with the composite assessment, activity 3.1c. Then answer these questions.

a. On which items were scores most closely aligned? (i.e. Creativity, Financial, Perseverance . . .)

b. On which items where there the greatest discrepancies in scores?

c. What surprises, if any, did you have?

B. Use feedback and insights. Using the information derived through this assessment, answer the following questions:

a. How will this information about your strengths and areas for development be helpful to you in planning your business?

b. How will this information be helpful to you in running your business?

c. Which, if any, of you strengths might afford you a competitive advantage in the marketplace?

C. **Plan steps to strengthen weak areas.** After reviewing the degree to which you possess entrepreneurial attributes, behaviors, and skills, which items will you seek to strengthen; and how will you do so?

D. **Identify professional expertise needed.** What type of outside expertise (i.e., accounting, marketing, information technology) will you likely need to hire?

Chapter 12

Evaluating Ideas: Personal, Professional & Financial Goals

In his book, *The Seven Habits of Highly Effective People*, Steven Covey states in Habit #2, "Begin with the End in Mind." This principle emphasizes that knowing where you want to end up provides guidance to you in your daily activities and decision making and enables you to accomplish your goals. Covey also says, "If your ladder is not leaning against the right wall, every step you take gets you to the wrong place faster." Both quotes speak to the importance of having clear goals for the future as a guide for present behavior.

PERSONAL AND PROFESSIONAL GOALS

Many books have been written on the importance of visioning and goal setting. By visualizing what you wish to accomplish and having clear goals to lead you in that direction, your actions will be more purposeful and productive.

It's important to frame having your own business in the context of having the life you wish to lead. A business is not an end in itself but rather a means to achieve that life. In Activity 3.3, you reflect on what you want your life to look like during the time you run your business and afterwards. What does personal and professional fulfillment mean to you? What will you be doing? Enjoying? Accomplishing? What will your lifestyle be? By answering these questions first, you can determine if the business idea(s) you have will lead to that life.

Another consideration you should factor into your goals is your desired level of physical and mental activity. In his article "7 Tips for Retirement Entrepreneurs," Mark Terry advises retirees, "Before starting a business, be realistic about the level of physical and mental energy you are willing or able to pour into your work. Some businesses can be run comfortably from your deck with a laptop computer and a cold beverage at your elbow. Others require significant physical labor—businesses such as a bakery, restaurant, or bed and breakfast."

The physical and mental demands of a business are important considerations for young entrepreneurs also. Their educational pursuits and/or family responsibilities are likely to impact the amount of time and energy they have available to run a business.

Sometimes the physical requirements of a job are not obvious. Factors such as heavy travel and a hectic schedule take their toll on a person's health and emotional wellbeing. Travel for personal pleasure is one thing; the pressure of standing in long airport lines and waiting for delayed flights while on a business trip is something entirely different. The money may not be enough to compensate for the stress and aggravation or what you are giving up—time with family or pursuing personal interests.

Long hours are another challenge. This is especially true in retail businesses, which are open twelve hours a day, six and a half days a week. It can be difficult to find good and reliable workers who are willing to work evenings and weekends. Business-to-business sales, rather than business-to-consumer sales, likely have more of an eight to five, five-day workweek, which allows more time for a personal life.

Taking into account travel, hours, and stress, many entrepreneurs opt for "lifestyle businesses" ones which afford them the opportunity to balance the demands of the business with their personal priorities.

_____

Mark Terry. "7 Tips for Retirement Entrepreneurs." *Bankrate.com.* Bankrate, 13 Sept. 2007. Web. 20 Sept. 2009.

Complete Activity 3.3, Screening: Personal and Professional Goals and Dreams, in which you look ahead and determine what you want your personal and professional lives to look like in the next 5, 10, and 20 years.

FINANCIAL GOALS

Closely aligned to your personal and professional goals are your financial goals, which you will clarify in Activity 3.4. Once again, money is not an end in itself but a means to an end—for you to have the life you want. Rarely do entrepreneurs cite money as the reason they started their businesses. They typically identify the desire to be their own boss and to pursue a passion as their motivations. Money is the by-product.

Although money may not be the primary motivator, it is important that the financial rewards of having your own business are adequate for the life you desire. To make this determination, it's important that you have a solid understanding of the financial potential of a proposed business.

Just as some careers provide more financial rewards than others, businesses also differ in the financial potential they provide. Knowing this proved beneficial to one middle-aged woman who was taking a Business Plan course and planning to open a candle shop in a local strip center. Detailed financial projections showed her that the most take-home income she could hope to make in her proposed venture was approximately $45,000 a year. Based on this analysis, she decided to wait to start a business until she came up with a business idea that would generate $80,000 a year. That was the amount she felt she needed to maintain her lifestyle and to compensate her for giving up her current job.

A good starting point to determining how much income you need to be able to take out of your business is to start by estimating your monthly expenses. This information will be helpful when you estimate yearly expenses in Activity 3.4, Screening: Financial Goals.

Pause and Reflect: Expenses	
Estimate the following expenses:	
Monthly Expenses	**Amount**
Clothes	$
Food—eating in	$

Food—eating out	$
Gas	$
Education	$
Entertainment	$
Insurances (other than medical)	$
Loans (other than car or house)	$
Medical Insurance	$
Payment (car)	$
Payment (mortgage) or Rent	$
Utilities	$
Other:	$
	$
	$
	$
TOTAL MONTHLY EXPENSES	$

FINANCIAL RISKS—HOW TO REDUCE THEM

Most start-up funding comes from the entrepreneur him/herself. You have to put some "skin in the game," as the saying goes. Yet many aspiring entrepreneurs do not have enough money to launch a business, and, even when they do, the money may be already earmarked to pay for the kids' college educations, purchase of a home, or fund retirement.

Options to obtain start-up funding include taking in investors or obtaining bank loans. Unless you have a proven track record, however, most investors must know you personally in order to put their hard-earned dollars in your hands. So if you plan to raise money by taking in investors, it's likely they are friends and family members, as is common in most start-up situations.

Insight or Common Sense
Limit your borrowing. Zero would be nice. Your chances of succeeding are better without carrying a large debt and interest burden.

If your business succeeds, everyone is happy. If things don't go well with your business, you may have to look at friends' and relatives' long faces and accusing eyes every Thanksgiving and Christmas for the rest of your life!

If you are able to attract professional investors and the business struggles or fails, you could lose it to unhappy stockholders if they muster the votes to replace you with someone they feel can lead the business more effectively.

If you borrow money and your business fails, you have a different problem. If you cannot repay your loan, the doors to your business may be closed by the courts. And if you have pledged personal assets such as a home as collateral for a loan, you could lose it as well.

Even if you decide you can handle the risks associated with borrowing capital, money may not be easy to find, especially with credit markets tightening due to the recent economic downturn. Banks are not willing to loan to businesses in the pre-revenue stage. In some cases, with an SBA loan guarantee, a bank will approve a loan. Seek out banks that work with SBA loan guarantee programs.

In recent years, the Web has provided an avenue to match those seeking funding with borrowers and investors. See "Funding from Strangers" for examples.

So both borrowing funds and taking in investors carry risks. But don't give up! Consider the following strategies that enable you to reduce the financial risks of starting your business:

Funding from Strangers

Get a Kick Start
www.Kickstarter.com is an online platform for funding both traditional and contemporary creative projects. Funding is for projects with definite timeframes (starting a business doesn't meet this criterion). Categories include Art, Dance, Design, Fashion, Film, Food, Games, Music, Photography, Publishing, Technology, Theater and more.

Prosper to Prosper
www.Prosper.com, an online peer-to-peer lending site in which people invest in each other, connects those in need of money with those who have money to loan. Borrowers then make fixed monthly payments to investors. "Roughly 14 percent of the money raised from the site is used for small-business capital, according to chief marketing officer Brad Lensing." ("Strangers with Money," *Entrepreneur* magazine. December 2012)

Note: These sites are included for informational purposes only. As with any business decision, obtain the appropriate expert, financial, and legal advice prior to proceeding.

- **Choose a Business with Low Start-Up Costs and Keep Expenses Low**
  Avoid businesses that require large investments in inventory, long-term leases, or building a facility. Many service, home-based, and online businesses are relatively inexpensive to start and can be self-financed.

It also goes without saying that you should minimize operating expenses whenever possible. In-home offices and virtual employees allow entrepreneurs to keep overhead and travel costs low.

- **Take in a Partner**
  You may want a partner for financial reasons or to share in the workload of the business. Read how this worked for sisters-in-law Renee and Kelly in "Combined Skills and Talents."

> **Combined Skills and Talents**
> Renee and Kelly, sisters-in-law, combined their artistic training, IT skills, and hobby of making jewelry to form a business selling jewelry through a Web site and at local events. Start up costs were minimal.

Partnerships, however, are not for everyone. Many partnerships dissolve as the business grows and different skill sets are needed. A written partnership agreement is a must. And make sure that the agreement includes the terms of how each partner can exit the partnership as well as how each partner's share of the business will be valued at the time of exit.

> **Insight or Common Sense**
> Look for compatibility in values and goals in choosing a partner.

- **Look for Industries with Higher-Than-Average Success Rates**
  Some industries have higher success rates than others. Choosing a business in one of these industries increases the odds in your favor from the start. For example, in his posting at www.smallbiztrends.com, Scott A. Shane, professor of entrepreneurial studies at Case Western Reserve University, states, "The data [from Amy Knaup of *Monthly Labor Review*] show that the four-year *survival rate* in the information sector is only 38 percent, but is 55 percent in the education and health services sector. That is, the average start-up in the education and health sector is 50 percent more likely than the average start-up in the information sector to live *(survive)* four years. That's a huge difference."[2]

In general, companies that sell to other businesses have a higher survival rate than those that sell directly to consumers. One reason cited for this is that

---

[2] (Start-Up Failure Rates Vary—Choosing the Right Industry Matters." <u>Small Business Trends</u>. Small Business Trends,. Web. 20 Sept. 2009)

entrepreneurs who start these businesses typically have considerable experience and knowledge of the industry, as opposed to consumer businesses which may attract those newer to the field.

- **Rethink Your Idea**

  Sometimes by even slightly altering your business concept, you can significantly reduce its start-up costs. For example, instead of opening a restaurant, which requires a huge capital investment, would you be happy with a catering business at a fraction of the start-up costs? This was the avenue followed by one Midwest barbeque restaurateur, whose early, loyal catering clients help fund his restaurant's startup.

  Instead of having a retail store, what about a kiosk in the mall or an online store? Start small and test the market for your products or services.

- **Start Your Business While Still Working**

  By continuing to work for someone else while running your own business on the side, you can reinvest any profits to fund your business's growth. You will be able to pay your bills without relying on your business for income. Working in your business part time also allows you to test the demand for your product or service.

Starting a business doesn't have to involve large financial risks. Think of steps you can take to reduce risks and record them in Pause and Reflect.

Pause and Reflect: Financial Risks
What steps can you take to minimize the financial risk of your business?

Student Workbook
In Activity 3.4, Screening: Financial Goals, identify your financial goals as well as the assets you have available to invest in your business.

3.3 activity
screening, personal and professional goals and dreams

Directions. Only you can evaluate whether or not your business will lead to personal and professional fulfillment. The first step in doing so is for you to visualize what personal and professional fulfillment looks like to you. Answering the following questions will help you do so.

A. My personal goals and dreams

a. Visualize your personal life in 5 years: How old will you be? _____
   Complete the following sentience: In 5 years I would like ....

b. Visualize your personal life in10 years. How old will you be? _____
   Complete the following sentience: In 10 years I would like .....

c. Visualize your personal life in 20 years. How old will you be? _____
   Complete the following sentience: In 20 years I would like ....

B. My professional goals and dreams

a. Visualize your professional life in 5 years. How old will you be? _____
   Complete the following sentience: In 5 years I would like ....

b. Visualize your professional life in 10 years. How old will you be? _____
   Complete the following sentience: In 10 years I would like ….

c. Visualize your professional life in 20 years. How old will you be? _____
   Complete the following sentience: In 20 years I would like ….

Synthesis goals and dreams screening

Of those ideas which best utilized your skills and talents, as identified in Activity 3.1, Matching Ideas with Skills and Characteristics, which one(s) are compatible with the personal and professional dreams and goals that you have noted in this activity. Rank order ideas as to their ability to meet your personal and professional goals and dreams.

Rank	Idea	Why Idea Select
1		
2		
3		

3.4

activity
screening, financial goals

A. My current financial NEEDS
I require the following income to support my current lifestyle. Do not include what others in your household may generate. Note: In Pause and Reflect in Chapter 12, you estimated your monthly expenses. This information will be helpful to you in determining your yearly financial needs.

( ) $0 - $25,000 per year   ( ) $26 - $50,000 per year
( ) $51 - $75,000 per year   ( ) $76 - $100,000 per year
( ) $101-$150,000   ( ) more than $151,000 per year

B. Future financial NEEDS
I need the following income to support my future lifestyle and goals.

( ) $0 - $25,000 per year   ( ) $26 - $50,000 per year
( ) $51 - $75,000 per year   ( ) $76 - $100,000 per year
( ) $101-$150,000   ( ) more than $151,000 per year

C. Future financial WANTS
I would like to have the following income to support my future lifestyle and goals.

( ) $0 - $25,000 per year   ( ) $26 - $50,000 per year
( ) $51 - $75,000 per year   ( ) $76 - $100,000 per year
( ) $101-$150,000   ( ) more than $151,000 per year

D. My personal net worth
Answer the following questions regarding your assets and liabilities.
Assets are items of value and may be liquid or fixed. Examples of **liquid assets** include cash (*money in checking or savings*) and near cash (*investments that can be readily converted into cash, like stocks and bonds*). Examples of **fixed assets** are your home and car.
Liabilities are claims against your assets, such as your home mortgage or what you owe the bank on your car.

1. My estimated liquid assets (cash/near cash) $_____
2. Other assets (estimate of real estate, cars, etc.) $_____
3. My estimated liabilities—what I owe. $_____
4. My total net worth   *$_____
   *Subtract your total liabilities (3) from your total assets (1 + 2).
   The remainder is your net worth.
5. I am willing to invest _____ percent of my net worth in
   my business. *Remember, not all of your net worth is liquid.*

6. Total amount in dollars I am willing to invest   *$_____
   Multiply your net worth, item 4, by the percentage you entered in item 5.

E. Other financial resources

Personal savings and money from family and friends (investments or loans) are the most common sources of start-up capital. In addition to what you are personally willing to invest in your business, what other funding can you obtain?

Source of Funding (List names or organizations.)	Approximate Amount
	$
	$
	$
	$
	$
TOTAL	$

F. Total amount of money from all sources $_____

Add together your total personal investment, item "D #6", and the total of other financial resources in "E" above.

G. Synthesis: Financial Needs and Goals Screening

Now that you have determined your financial resources and goals, evaluate the business ideas listed in Activity 3.3, item "C," to identify which have the potential of meeting your financial needs. For those which do, list them here in rank order.

Rank	Idea	Why Idea Selected
1		
2		
3		

H. Based on item "F" above (total amount of money from all sources) which of the businesses listed do you have the financial resources to start? Identify them here:

_____

_____

Chapter 13

Evaluating Ideas: Market Viability

At the center of an opportunity is an idea, but not all ideas are opportunities. Market viability is the litmus test for determining if a business idea is really a business opportunity. Ask yourself, "Does a market exist for the product or service I am considering? Will anyone want to buy it? These are questions you'll want to consider in determining the market viability of your business.

Look around you for evidence of market acceptance of your idea. This evidence might include identifying others who are successfully offering your product or service. It might include identifying potential customers who are ready and willing to buy.

But to answer these questions confidently, you may need to conduct some basic market research. Research doesn't have to be difficult. Every time you google a topic, you're conducting research.

In this chapter, you'll learn about conducting market research using secondary sources in which you search for answers in existing data. In Chapter 14, you'll conduct primary research in which you gather data that has not previously existed. Primary research is typically done when no secondary sources can be found for the type of data that is needed. Common primary research methods include surveys, interviews, and focus groups.

MARKET RESEARCH USING SECONDARY SOURCES

There are a multitude of secondary research sources, including magazines and newspapers, books, journals, Web sites, and government publications. Secondary data can be especially helpful in determining the condition of your industry—its growth potential, major trends, and the competitive environment. Read in "Market Research Led to Winning Idea" how the research Delena Stout conducted led to her unique and successful business. Similar to Delena's experience, the information you gather through research will be invaluable to your business.

Although secondary research is the easiest and least expensive to gather, it has some drawbacks. It may not provide the most current data or be exactly what you need.

For convenience and because of the amount of information available, use the Internet to start your research. Search engines are easy to use, and you can refine your search by using the "Advance Search" feature. Many databases are available online. Some require a subscription fee, but many are free.

Market Research Led to Winning Idea

Delena Stout, founder of Brookside Barkery and Bath (see Featured Entrepreneur in Chapter 10), used market research to fine-tune her original business concept. Her research revealed that her initial idea, a place to bathe dogs, was not profitable enough to meet her financial goals. Research into trends in the pet industry and her interest in the health of her own dogs led her to add pet nutrition to her initial idea of a place to bathe dogs.

Consider this word of caution, however, about relying on information obtained through the Internet. Just as with any information you obtain, carefully assess the reliability of the source of the information and look for consistency among various sources.

Your local library also has helpful reference sources and current information. Don't be reluctant to ask for a librarian's assistance in tracking down information; that's his or her job. Years of experience and technical know-how typically allow a librarian to quickly locate a desired resource rather than using the Alice-in-Wonderland approach common to the inexperienced researcher.

Plan Your Research. As with most events in life, things go better with a plan. Follow these three steps to make the most of your research time and efforts.

1. **Set your research goals**. Because of the sheer volume of information available, the success of using secondary sources hinges on the clarity of your research goals. These may be worded as goals or as questions to be answered. As one market

research specialist stated, "You need to ask the right questions; finding the answers is the easy part."

Obviously, some information is more critical to entrepreneurial decision making than others. A piece of information of significant importance is the potential sales for a particular type of business. This information is often difficult to ascertain since sales information is not readily available on small businesses. To estimate sales, you will likely have to extrapolate from data about the sales volume of large businesses, national or aggregate sales numbers, and sales trends.

One helpful resource is *Dun and Bradstreet Key Business Ratios*, which is found in most libraries and includes averages of the financial data of small, medium, and large business reported by SIC Code. These sales and expense averages provide start-up businesses sound data on which to base their projections and save a lot of guesswork.

2. **Conduct research**. Before starting, consider the types of resources available. In addition to those already mentioned—Web sites, journals, articles, government data—it is helpful to connect with a trade association in your field if you have not already done so. This will allow you to gain access to their latest research as well as help you meet members, another excellent source of information. To find relevant trade associations, check the *Encyclopedia of Associations* found in most libraries or you can google for a relevant trade association.

3. **Compile and interpret data.** Once you have gathered information related to your research goals, it is time to reflect on it with a discerning eye. Look for similarities, differences, and data trends. In research, quality and quantity matter.

INDUSTRY RESEARCH

You may be very familiar with the industry in which your business will operate, as you have worked in it and can easily answer questions about its *size and growth potential* and identify *trends* impacting it. If the industry in which your business will operate is new to you, however, it will take a concerted effort on your part to find this information.

When conducting industry research, follow these steps:
1. Look at the big picture first—how is the industry doing on a national or international level. Industry information can be found on the Internet and in most

business libraries. Start by googling "industry outlook xxx," replacing "xxx" with the name of your industry.

Secondary data found in libraries and on the Web is often reported by NAICS (North American Industry Classification System) codes or SIC (Standard Industrial Classification) codes. NAICS is the newer classification system and lists more of the technology and service businesses prevalent today.

- To find your NAIC code, go to the U.S. Census NAICS Web site at http://www.census.gov/naics. On the left-hand side of the page, enter your industry name in the space that says "enter key word"; you may need to try several variations of it before being able to identify a classification that aptly describes your industry.

- You can research your SIC Code by going to the key word search area of the U.S. Department of Labor Web site at http://www.osha.gov/pls/imis/sicsearch.html.

- Or you can try to find your code through Google or another search engine by typing in NAICS or SIC and your type of business. For example, you might type in "NAICS environmental consulting." If doing so doesn't provide the results you want, think of your business in terms of its broader category to find a relevant code. For example, instead of environmental consulting, you might google "NAICS consulting."

These codes will be helpful in finding industry information in various resources, such as the *Encyclopedia of American Industries* and *Standard & Poor's Industry Surveys*. Most business libraries also subscribe to the Business and Company Database. On it, click on Industry Search at top of screen and enter your industry's NAICS or SIC Code. The more closely the NAICS/SIC code title describes your industry, the more useful the information.

Identifying an industry trade association related to your type of business may provide you access to information and individuals who can help you determine your industry's growth potential, trends, and regulations. To identify a relevant trade association, check the *Encyclopedia of Associations* available in most libraries or google "xxx association," substituting the name of your industry for the "xxx's."

Step 2. Then focus on the smaller picture—market demand for your product or service within your specific trade area. This information can be a more challenging to obtain as there may be an absence of existing research on local or regional markets. Some counties collect data related to local demographics and businesses and some chambers of commerce do so as well.

You may need to conduct your own market research—surveying potential customers, talking with suppliers, and assessing local economic conditions and zip code demographics to gather this data. More is written on how to conduct primary research in Chapter 14.

Sales and customer demand are not the only considerations in assessing market potential. If you are selling through distributors or wholesalers, you also need to take into account how open and welcoming they are to new suppliers. The Internet, which enables entrepreneurs to sell directly to the public, has helped many entrepreneurs address the problem of unwelcoming distribution channel members.

COMPETITIVE RESEARCH

Early in the planning process is the time to look at the competitive environment and key competitors. If these competitors are local establishments, visit them. If not, examine your competitors' Web sites and talk to customers, suppliers, or others familiar with the businesses.

You may also be able to research information about competitors online. Detailed geographic, industry, and other information for U.S. business establishments can be found at www.census.gov/econ/cbp/index.html

Another helpful Web site for information on businesses is www.manta.com. On this site, you can search by type of businesses and location (city or zip code). Information is provided by business category as well as by individual business, including revenue, date started, number of employees, and contact person. To obtain information, you are required to sign up. At the date of this writing, there is no charge to do so, but be sure to determine this prior to signing up.

Sorkins Directory of Business and Government provides detailed information on public and private companies, non-profit organizations, and government agencies, and can be a helpful resource for collecting information about local and regional businesses. Check with your local library for this resource.

If you own a retail business, check out your competition in your local *Yellow Pages* (paper edition) or at www.Yellowpages.com . Your local librarian may also be able to point you to resources for information on area businesses.

In addition to the number of competitors in the field, identify their basis for competition. Is it quality? Price? Location? Efficient delivery? Service? Then determine how you will compete with these more established businesses. Another me-too business will have difficulty attracting customers.

How much research is enough? That is a hard question to answer and one you will have to decide for yourself. Information helps overcome fear. The more information you have, the more confident you will be in your decision about whether or not to start your business.

In Chapter 16 you complete an Environmental Scan and a Competitive Scan to examine the marketing conditions surrounding your business (idea).

ADDITIONAL RESOURCES
In addition to secondary sources—research that has already been conducted—and primary research—which you conduct yourself—consider the follow options to help you answer important marketing questions related to your business:
- Contact your local Small Business Development Center (SBDC) located on the campuses of many colleges or universities. They provide free consulting to aspiring and early growth entrepreneurs.
- Contact the Service Core of Retired Executives (SCORE) available at many Small Business Administration (SBA) offices. They provide free consulting.

- Hire a marketing consultant, particularly one with experience working with your type of business.
- Take a class or read some of the numerous books on marketing, including ones on bootstrap or guerilla marketing and no- or low-cost ways to promote your business.

After identifying your number one business idea in Activity 3.5, Screening: Market Viability Scorecard, you will use the techniques and resources identified in this chapter to conduct environmental and competitive scans in Chapter 16. You may wish to revisit your Market Viability Scorecard after doing so.

Student Workbook
Complete Activity 3.5, Screening: Market Viability Scorecard. In it you will identify the business idea (two if ideas are tied) that rated the highest for market viability and begin your research by identifying a NAIC/SIC code and professional association related to it.

At this point, you will have evaluated the business ideas you identified in Steps 1 and 2 against your skills and talents, dreams and goals, and the marketplace. Finally, in Activity 3.6, you describe the ONE business idea that best withstood the scrutiny of the screening process conducted in Step 3. Then in Activity 3.7 you scan the marketplace to determine if this idea is "on trend," if it capitalizes upon one or more marketplace trends, or if it can be altered or refined to do so.

Student Workbook
Complete Activity 3.6, Your #1 Idea—The Shoe that Fits, and Activity 3.7, Supporting Trends for #1 Idea.

STEP 3: INTRODUCTION TO FEATURED ENTREPRENEUR
The combined talents of Elizabeth Erlandson and partner Ardith Stuertz enabled them to launch and grow Licorice International into a thriving online mail order and retail business.

Featured Entrepreneur Elizabeth Erlandson, Licorice International
Online mail order business and retail store

For Elizabeth Erlandson and Ardith Stuertz, owners of Licorice International, the caveat not to go into business with friends did not hold true. For some time, Elizabeth and Ardith knew they wanted to start a business together. They carefully assessed the skills each brought to the table and prayed for guidance in their choice of business. Their initial joint endeavor was a consulting firm for non-profits that capitalized on their accounting, human resources, and public relations backgrounds, **"building on what we knew,"** stated Elizabeth. "The secret of our successful partnership was common core values and mutual respect, a must for a successful long-term business relationship," Elizabeth shared.

Their consulting business afforded Elizabeth and Ardith the opportunity to work together as partners, develop new skills and business contacts, and find out what they really enjoyed doing. It also brought home the fact that their business's growth was limited by the number of hours they had available to work. "In consulting, you sell your time," Elizabeth stated. Concluding they **needed a product to sell**, they were inspired by the story, "Acres of Diamonds," included on page 28 to **look in their backyard** for their diamond—a winning product.

Researching what made a product successful, Elizabeth concluded they were looking for **"something people wanted that wasn't readily available."** Licorice candy fit the bill, as Elizabeth knew from looking for good black licorice for her husband over the years. Her mother-in-law, Anna, found a small mail order business which she frequently ordered her son's favorites. When Anna moved into a nursing home and stopped supplying these tasty goodies, her son, Doug, shared an old order form

Ardith Stuertz and Elizabeth Erlandson

with his wife so she could "surprise" him. She did better than that . . . she bought the business (along with her husband and their good friends, Ardith and John).

Since its founding in 2002, several moves have allowed Licorice International to continue to grow to its present retail location of 4,450 square feet in Lincoln, Nebraska's historic Haymarket district. They offer over 160 types of licorice from 13 countries.

In terms of the future, Elizabeth said, "Both of us want to do **philanthropic work,** so we are waiting to decide if we want to continue to develop the business, grow it to the next level—which would take an infusion of cash and talent—or sell the business. I am not ready for retirement."

You can find more information on Licorice International by visiting their Web site at www.licoriceinternational.com

3.5

activity
screening, market
viability scorecard

Directions. Complete the following Market Viability Scorecards for up to three ideas identified in the Synthesis section (item G) of activity 3.4. Answer questions "Yes" or "No" based on your current knowledge of the marketplace. (Note: If you prepare a Business Plan for your business idea after the conclusion of this course, the research you conduct will enable you to more definitively answer these questions.)

A. Idea #1 _____

#	Yes	No	Question
1.			Is there a perceived need for this product or service?
2.			Is there a clearly identified target market (those to whom you plan to sell that can be described by market segmentation factors)? If yes, describe here:
3.			Does the target market have the ability to buy your product or service at a price that will provide an adequate profit?
4.			Does the marketplace need another provider of this product or service?
5.			Is the demand for this product or service relatively strong?
6.			Are the growth projections for sales strong?
7.			Will you have a sustainable competitive advantage (something in which you excel)? If yes, what is it?
8.			Is there strong evidence of market acceptance of the product or service? If yes, what is it?
9.			Do you have the ability to produce and sell enough of the product or service to be a profitable business?
10.			Is there a way to easily reach the targeted market?
Tot.			**Total number of "x's" in each column and record total here.**

B. Idea #2 _____

#	Yes	No	Question
1.			Is there a perceived need for this product or service?
2.			*Is there a clearly identified target market (those to whom you plan to sell that can be described by market segmentation factors)? If yes, describe here:*
3.			*Does the target market have the ability to buy your product or service at a price that will provide an adequate profit?*
4.			*Does the marketplace need another provider of this product or service?*
5.			*Is the demand for this product or service relatively strong?*
6.			*Are the growth projections for sales strong?*
7.			*Will you have a sustainable competitive advantage (something in which you excel)? If yes, what is it?*

8.			*Is there strong evidence of market acceptance of the product or service? If yes, what is it?*
9.			*Do you have the ability to produce and sell enough of the product or service to be a profitable business?*
10.			*Is there a way to easily reach the targeted market?*
Tot.			**Total number of "x's" in each column and record total here.**

C.   Idea #3 _____

#	Yes	No	Question
1.			Is there a perceived need for this product or service?
2.			Is there a clearly identified target market (those to whom you plan to sell that can be described by market segmentation factors)? If yes, describe here:
3.			Does the target market have the ability to buy your product or service at a price that will provide an adequate profit?
4.			Does the marketplace need another provider of this product or service?
5.			Is the demand for this product or service relatively strong?
6.			Are the growth projections for sales strong?
7.			Will you have a sustainable competitive advantage (something in which you excel)? If yes, what is it?
8.			Is there strong evidence of market acceptance of the product or service? If yes, what is it?
9.			Do you have the ability to produce and sell enough of the product or service to be a profitable business?
10.			Is there a way to easily reach the targeted market?
Tot.			**Total number of "x's" in each column and record total here.**

Synthesis of market viability

Identify the business idea that scored highest on the Market Viability Scorecard (most "X's" in the "yes" column), and start your secondary research by identifying a NAICS/SIC code and professional association for this type of business. Contact association now for information on trends and growth, which will be needed in upcoming activities. .Note: *Market research will need to be undertaken to obtain an accurate picture of the market viability of your business idea. Completing the Market Viability Scorecard here prompts you to begin thinking about key market variables.*

#1 Business Idea (If two ideas are tied, list both)	NIACS/ SIC Code	Professional Association

3.6

activity
your #1 idea –
the shoe that fits

Directions.   Which business idea most successfully completed the screening process?   This is "the shoe that fits," the key to your entrepreneurial future.

The Shoe That Fits is: _____

a. Describe your **#1** business idea briefly. What will your product or service look like?

b. How do you feel about starting this type of business (i.e. excited? comfortable? knowledgeable? apprehensive?)?

c. What other ideas (from previous lists) will you keep as backup?

	Back Up Ideas
1	
2	
3	

3.7 activity
supporting trends
for #1 idea

Directions. For your #1 idea, scan various printed sources and the Internet to identify trends that indicate that the time is right for your business.

	Supporting Trend	**Source** *Name, Date, (i.e. article, web site)*
1		
2		
3		

Step 4

Further Investigation and Getting Started

Step 4 Objective

To research your #1 business idea and take strategic steps to launch your business by

- Surveying members of your target market.
- Conducting a competitive scan and an environmental scan.
- Developing a Business Concept Statement.
- Identifying first customers.
- Networking for success.

© Achēve Consulting Inc.

Chapter 14

Further Investigation

As you saw when you completed the market viability scorecard in the last chapter, without hard data you are making an educated guess, at best, as to the market's response to your product or service. This experience likely illustrated to you the need for factual information on which to base your decisions. Identifying your NAICS or SIC code in Activity 3.5 and a professional trade association in a Pause and Reflect activity in Chapter 13 were positive steps toward starting your research with secondary data. But secondary research may not be enough.

The greater the risks associated with starting a business, the greater the need for hard data and the more extensive the research required. Even for supposedly low-risk ventures, such as bookkeeping or child care services, there are hidden costs in terms of lost time, energy, and income. And that doesn't account for the psychic costs of starting a business that fails. With that in mind, all concepts warrant careful investigation.

Being calculated risk takers, entrepreneurs are looking for verification that they should proceed with their plans. Success at each step, and targeted research regarding the next one, propels entrepreneurs from one stage of business development to another.

In the previous chapter, you looked at how to conduct market research using secondary resources, existing data from government agencies, chambers of commerce, educational institutions, industry and trade associations, and media and commercial sites. In this chapter you will conduct primary market research, original research specifically for your business.

This research will help you more clearly define your business idea and transform it into a Business Concept Statement. According to Dictionary.com, an *idea* is "your intention; what you intend to do." A *concept* is "a scheme; a plan." Converting an idea (intention) into a concept (plan) takes research. The Business Concept Statement, which you prepare in the next chapter, not only identifies your product or service, but to whom you plan to sell, why they will buy from you, and how you will promote and distribute your product.

> *"Basic research is what I am doing when I don't know what I am doing."*
> Wernher von Braun

In this chapter you conduct primary research by surveying members of your target market. Following is a brief overview of target markets, which was addressed earlier in Chapter 9.

TARGET MARKETS

Most successful small businesses use a targeted marketing strategy for reaching customers, as opposed to a mass marketing strategy that may be used by larger businesses. By narrowly identifying target markets, they can ensure that their products meet their customers' needs and more effectively promote their products to potential customers.

Be cautious if you think "**everyone**" is your target market. What products appeal to "everyone" equally? What this typically means is that the entrepreneur has not done the research to more clearly identify who will most likely purchase from them. Market segmentation factors, such as the following, have a strong influence on what customers buy.

> **Home Builder Targets Baby Boomers**
> Home builder Gary Ramariz's garden villas were targeted to the aging baby boomer population interested in downsizing after their children left home. His maintenance-provided community allowed these boomers time to travel and pursue hobbies. Even though he was a boomer himself, Gary conducted market research to ensure he was meeting this market's unique needs. Previously he had sold primarily to first-time home buyers or young families with children.

Market Segmentation

First consider whether yours is a consumer market, in which individuals and households purchase for their own use, or a business market, in which purchases are made for resale or to be used in the production of a product. In some cases, you may sell to both.

Then break target markets down further by identifying other segmentation factors which influence the purchase of your product or service. Common segmentation factors, as shown in Diagram 2.1 earlier in the book, include the following:

Consumer Market (Business-to-Consumer)
Geographic (where buyers are located)
Demographic factors (i.e., age, gender, income, ethnicity, education)
Psychographic factors (i.e., motives for buying, patterns of buying, personality traits, lifestyle)

Business Market (Business-to-Business)
Geographic (location)
Demographic (size, sales, industry)
Buying patterns

In many cases, there are several target markets to which you might sell. If so, your initial challenge becomes one of prioritizing. To which market should your initial sales and marketing efforts be addressed? In making this determination, consider sales and profit potential, the competitive environment, and your ability to reach each market.

Now visualize the primary target market for your business and describe it below, recognizing that your answers to these questions may change as a result of the research you conduct in this chapter.

Pause and Reflect: Consumer or Business Target Market Will I sell my product to a consumer market or a business market? **Circle** either "Consumer" or "Business" below and then respond to the appropriate set of questions.	
Consumer	Business
For potential customers: • In what geographic area do they reside? • What age range is representative of the **majority** of them? • What income level is representative of the **majority** of them? • What is their most typical lifestyle? • What is their mindset?	For potential customers: • In what geographic area are they located? • In what industry(ies) are the majority? • What is the typical size of business (i.e. number of employees, revenue)?

Later, when completing your own primary research in Activity 4.1, you should make every effort to survey respondents that closely resemble the target market you described here.

PRIMARY MARKET RESEARCH

Not all the information you need will be readily available to you. Sometimes, the only way to find it is to gather it yourself—to conduct primary research. To do so, you may need the assistance of those trained in research techniques, as may be the case in conducting interviews or focus groups.

Primary Research Methods

There are many ways you can collect information. Key research methods include interviews, observation, focus groups, and surveys/questionnaires. For example, if you plan to open a high-end hair salon, potential primary research methods include

- Interviewing potential clients one-on-one.
- Observing customers' behaviors and purchases while they receive services at competitors' shops.
- Observing customers as they enter and exit competitors' shops, noting demographic and psychographic factors.
- Holding a focus group of anywhere from 8 – 12 potential clients to obtain their input and opinions.
- Surveying potential customers by asking them a series of structured questions.

In this chapter, you will learn more about how to conduct a survey and develop one to gather information from a small but representative group of potential customers for your business. A word of caution, however. Making decisions based on a small survey group's responses is risky. A larger number of survey responses are needed and/or supporting research gathered through other sources to make valid decisions.

Survey Content

Just as when conducting secondary research, you need to identify the goals you hope to accomplish when conducting primary research. The primary goal of the survey you will conduct in this chapter is to obtain feedback on your business concept.

Some nascent entrepreneurs are very uncomfortable with sharing their business idea with others at this point for fear someone will steal it. This is sometimes referred to as "entrepreneurial paranoia," for lack of a better term. Although you may have a legitimate concern and need to take reasonable steps to protect your idea, this concern can hinder your obtaining valuable marketplace input. See the "Entrepreneurial Paranoia" textbox for more discussion on the topic.

Once you've decided it's okay to talk to others and solicit feedback, with whom will you talk? Family members? Friends? What you will likely hear from these respondents is what a great idea you have. Either they don't want to hurt your feelings or they feel they are not qualified to judge the value of your business idea.

So how do you gather *objective* feedback on your business idea? One very helpful tool is to survey your target market—the customer group to which you plan to sell.

Entrepreneurial Paranoia

What if you tell others and someone steals your idea? This is a common concern of entrepreneurs and, in rare cases, a legitimate one. Take reasonable steps to protect your idea by not sharing it with individuals who have almost identical skills as yours, can easily replicate it, and are interested in doing so. Also be sure to protect any intellectual property you might have. For most entrepreneurs, however, operating in a vacuum poses a much greater risk than having their idea stolen. At some point in the future, your business will go public (open its doors). At that time, everyone will have access to your business information.

Insight or Common Sense
Feedback at this stage in the entrepreneurial planning process is critical. Decisions made while your idea is still on the drawing board are cheap!

In your survey, you will attempt to find out what features are important to your buyers and what benefits are valued. For example, the features of the watch on your wrist might include 14K solid gold link band, mother-of-pearl dial, Swiss quartz movements, numbered face, time and date, and so on. The benefits depend to some extent on the buyer but would likely include convenience, dependability, and style. Customers buy benefits; many entrepreneurs, especially inexperienced ones, think in terms of features.

Other questions you want answered through your surveys are
- What marketing methods would be most effective in reaching potential customers?
- How sensitive are buyers to price?
- What does your typical customer look like (demographic/psychographic characteristics)?

Cautiously examine all feedback you receive. Look for patterns. If the survey is taken orally, LISTEN carefully to respondents' inferences and emotions. It may be more telling than the words they actually say.

"The next best thing to always being right is
to find out you are wrong very quickly."
John Manley

You'll also want to back up your survey results by talking with suppliers, other entrepreneurs, and business advisors such as those available through your local SBDC or SCORE offices.

To help you in preparing your written survey in Activity 4.2, you will first test it by administering it orally to a small number of people in Activity 4.1. Then, after making the revisions to the survey that this test suggests, you prepare a written version to administer to a larger number of members of your target market. Following is an example of how this written survey might appear for a home accessories and design shop. (Note: This survey could be printed one-sided on a piece of 8 ½ x 17 legal sized paper.)

CrystalPlume
Home Décor and More

A. DESCRIPTION. CrystalPlume is a one-stop shopping haven offering unique, eclectic, and quality accents and accessories for the entire home, as well as in-store and in-home design assistance to the style-conscious consumer. Unique wall décor, lamps, furniture and seasonal merchandise allows clients to express their own creativity or work with highly regarded designers to create homes of their dreams. Personalized service, a convenient location, and home delivery ensures customers an enjoyable, productive shopping experience.

1. Would you purchase this product or service? ___ Yes___ No
   If **no**, "Why not?" Record your answer here.

   Even if you answered "No" to the question above, please complete this survey.

B. FEATURES. Following is a list of possible features that CrystalPlume may include. Please indicate with a checkmark (√) the top five (5) you would purchase/use.

___ Lamps	___Window treatments	___ Wall decor
___ Chairs	___ Seasonal Decor	___ Candles
___ Area rugs	___ Original art	___ In-store design assistance
___ Pillows	___ Bar stools	___ In-home design assistance

What other features (if any) would you like to see included? _____

C. BENEFITS. Following is a list of potential benefits of visiting CrystalPlume and purchasing their merchandize and/or using their design services. Please indicate with a checkmark (√) the top three (3) benefits of doing so.
___ Convenience of one stop for decorating needs
___ Variety of high quality, unique décor items
___ Potential cost savings over purchasing through individual vendors.
___ Personal service of talented, in-store staff.
___ Time savings in identifying and locating a design professional (in-store designer)
___ Time savings and confidence in contacting a vetted design professional for in-home help.
What other benefits (if any) do you anticipate? _____

D. MARKETING. Following is a list of possible marketing methods. Please indicate with a checkmark (√) the three (3) that would be most effective in reaching you.

___ Phonebook/Yellow Pages	___ Local newspapers	___ Internet/Email
___ Local home shows	___ Local/regional magazines	___ Presentations to groups
___ Flyers	___ Radio/Television	___ Event/charity sponsorship
___Articles (décor tips) in publication	___ Free classes on decorating	___ Newsletters

What other marketing method would be effective in reaching you and others?

E. PRICING. Because of the quality and uniqueness of CrystalPlume merchandize, it would use a premium pricing strategy, positioning itself high (but not the highest) in the relevant price range. With this pricing structure, would you purchase at CrystalPlume?

If you answered "No", what would justify CrystalPlume charging a premium price?

F. QUANTITY. Approximately how many purchases would you make in a year?

G. DEMOGRAPHIC INFORMATION. Please provide the following information

1.Age	2. Ethnic Background	3. Employment Status
o Less than 25	o African American	o Full-time
o 25-34	o American Indian	o Part-time
o 35-44	o Asian or Pacific Islander	o Homemaker/Stay-at-home

o 45-54 o 55-64 o 65 or older	o Caucasian o Hispanic o Other	parent o Student o Not employed o Retired
4.Gender o Male o Female	5.Residential Status o Own o Rent	6.Marital Status o Single o Married o Divorced /Widowed
7. Yearly Income o Less than $25,000 o $26-50,000 o $51-80,000 o $81-120,000 o $121-150,000 o $151-200,000 o Over $200,000	8.Education Completed o High School or less o Some college o College degree o Graduate	9. How many people live in your household? Adults o 1-2 o 3 or more Children o 1 or more
When CrystalPlume opens, would you like to be contacted? ___Yes ___ No If yes, please provide name, phone number, and e-mail below.		
Thank you for your assistance with this survey! *Please use the enclosed stamped, self-addressed envelope to return it.*		

You may recall that entrepreneur Susan Davidson, Featured Entrepreneur at the end of Chapter 5, surveyed international managers and expatriates and their family members to gather information about her prospective business consulting clients and their needs. Susan conducted an online survey with 63 international professionals, followed by in-depth telephone interviews with 32 of the respondents prior to beginning her business, Beyond Borders.

As response rates to surveys vary drastically depending on whom you survey—their level of interest in your product or service and their relationship to you—you may need to survey many people to obtain the number of responses desired.

Start early in developing and administering your survey as it typically takes more time than expected to gather survey results.

Student Workbook
Complete Activity 4.1, Concept Testing—Oral Survey, which will help you prepare the written survey you will disseminate in Activity 4.2, Concept Testing—Written Survey.

4.1 activity concept testing – oral survey overview

Directions

1. **Prepare Oral Survey.** Using your #1 idea identified in Step 3, you will test your business concept by asking several individuals who are likely future customers for feedback.

   Utilize the following format to develop an oral survey, which will be used as the basis for the written survey you will develop and administer in activity 4.2. Your oral survey will include the following:
   - **Description of product or service.** Start with a brief, written description of your product or service as you envision it.
   - **Features and benefits.** Ask potential customers what features are important to them? For those they name, ask why they are important? What benefits do they provide?
   - **Method of promotion.** Ask how they (or others) would locate your type of business or product. Would they look in the phone book? Look at ads? Ask others for a recommendation? Ask how they (and others) will purchase your product or service (i.e. retail location, Internet, order direct)
   - **Pricing.** Ask potential customers what they would be willing to pay. *Note: Questions regarding price can assist you in quantifying the perceived value of your product to buyers. It can also help you determine if you can sell your product or service at a profit.*
   - **Demographic data.** Collect information from respondents about <u>relevant</u> demographic variables (i.e. age, gender, profession, income, education).

2. **Complete the top portions of sections** "A," "B," "C," "D," and "E" on form 4.1a, oral survey, interviewer's leads.

3. **Interview three individuals** (noting their names, positions, and relationship to you) by reading the survey leads for sections "A," "B," "C," "D," and "E and asking the survey questions that follow in each section.

2. **Record respondents' answers** on form 4.1b.

3. **Upon completion, obtain respondents' feedback** on the clarity and content of the entire survey.

   Note: Survey responses don't necessary predict actual consumer behavior. The true test is not what people say but whether or not they will open their billfolds and make purchases.

4.1a activity concept testing – oral survey interviewer's leads

Directions. Complete the TOP portion of each item below by recording your responses on the lines provided. The bottom portion of each item is shown for information purposes only. Record respondent's answers on one of the three copies of form 4.1b provided.

Respondent #1 (Identify name, position, relationship to you.)

_____

A. Description. Briefly describe your product or service below.

_____
_____
_____

Record respondent's answers on form 4.1b.
A. Read product/service description to respondent and ask respondent following questions.
1. Would you purchase this product or service? ___ Yes___ No
   If **no**, ask, "Why not?" and record response here.
   *** *Even if respondent answered "No" to the question above, have him/her complete survey.* ***

B. Features. Features are specific parts or components of your product or service. List significant ones here. *(You may need to expand listing beyond 5.)*
1.
_____
2.
_____
3.
_____
4.
_____
5.
_____

Record respondent's answers on form 4.1b.
B. Share product/service features with respondent and ask the following questions.
1. Which features are most valuable to you (or other customers) and why?
2. What other features would you like to see included?

C. Benefits. List key benefits to customers. *(You may need to expand listing beyond 4..)*
1._____
2._____
3._____
4._____

> **Record respondent's answers on form 4.1b.**
> C. Share product/service benefits with respondent and ask the following questions.
> 1. Which benefits are of greatest value to you (or other customers) and why?
> 2. Are there other benefits that I have not identified?

D. Marketing Methods. List types of marketing planned (sales, advertising, and promotion).

_____

_____

_____

_____

> **Record respondent's answers on form 4.1b.**
> D. Share marketing methods above and ask respondent the following questions.
> 1. Which marketing methods would be most effective in reaching you?
>   _(How would you [or others] expect to find out about my product or service?)_
> 2. What other marketing methods would you suggest?

E. Pricing. Indicate the price or price range (low, medium, or high relative to similar products or services in the market) you plan to charge. _____

> **Record respondent's answers on form 4.1b.**
> E. **Pricing.** Share price/price range (low, mid, high) with respondent and ask the following:
> **If Specific Price:**
> 1. At this _price,_ would you/others buy this product?   ___ Yes ___No
> 2. If **yes,** ask, "Would you buy at an even higher price?"   ___Yes ___ No
> 3. If **yes,** ask, "How much is the most you would be willing to pay?" _____
> 4. If **no,** ask, "What would justify my charging this price?
> **If Price Range**
> 1. With this pricing strategy, would you purchase this product/service?
> 2. What factors would justify my charging a higher price (or positioning my product/service higher in the price range)?

> **F. Quantity**
> Ask, "Approximately how many purchases of this product or service would you make in a year?" _Note: Omit this question if purchase would likely be a one-time event._
> **Record respondent's answers on form 4.1b.**

G. Demographic information about respondent
Insert questions about <u>relevant</u> demographic information on respondents, i.e. age (give ranges), number of family members living in household, location, income (give ranges), education, etc. _Remember, respondents are more apt to answer questions of a personal nature, like age or income, if they are given ranges to which to respond._
1._____
2._____
3._____
4._____

> **Record Respondent's answers on form 4.1b.**
> G. **Demographic information.** Ask questions listed above and record respondents' answers

4.1b activity concept testing – oral survey responses

Directions. Share information included on 4.1a, interviewer's leads, with respondent (previous two pages). Record respondent's answers here.

Respondent #1 (name, position, relationship to you.) _____

_____

A. Description. Read product/service description to respondent (from lined section of item "A" if 4.1a) and ask respondent the following questions.

1. Would you purchase this product or service?   ___ Yes___ No

If **no**, ask, "Why not?"and record response here.
*** *Even if respondent answered "No" to the question above, have them complete survey.* ***

B. Features. Share product/service features (from lined section of item "B" in 4.1a) with respondent and ask the following questions.

1. Which features are most valuable to you (or other customers) and why?

2. What other features would you like to see included?

C. Benefits. Share product/service benefits with respondent (from lined section of item "C" inn 4.1a) and ask the following questions.

1. Which benefits are of greatest value to you (or other customers) and why?

2. Are there other benefits that I have not identified?

D. Marketing. Share marketing methods (from lined section of item "D" in 4.1a) and ask respondent the following questions.

1. Which marketing methods would be most effective in reaching you?
    (How would you [or others] expect to find out about my product or service?)

2. What other marketing methods would you suggest?

E. Pricing. Share price/price range (from item "E" in 4.1a) with respondent and ask the following questions.

If Specific Price:
1. At this *price,* would you/others buy this product?   ___ Yes ___No
2. If yes, ask, "Would you buy at an even higher price?"   ___ Yes ___ No
3. If yes, ask, "How much is the most you would be willing to pay?" _____
4. If no, ask, "What would justify my charging this price?" _____

If Price Range
1. With this pricing strategy, would you purchase this product/service?

2. What factors would justify my charging a higher price (or positioning my product higher in the price range)?

F. Quantity.
Ask, "Approximately how many purchases of this product or service would you make in a year?" *Note: Omit this question if purchase would likely be a one-time event.*

G. Demographic information. Ask questions listed on lined section of item "G" in 4.1a and record respondent's answers here.

4.1b activity
concept testing –
oral survey responses

Directions. Share information included on original survey form with respondent (from "oral survey—interviewer's leads" on previous two pages. Record respondents answers here.

Respondent #2 (name, position, relationship to you.) _____
_____

A. Description. Read product/service description to respondent (from lined section of item "A" if 4.1a) and ask respondent the following questions.
1. Would you purchase this product or service?   ___ Yes___ No

   If **no**, ask, "Why not?"and record response here.
   *** *Even if respondent answered "No" to the question above, have them complete survey.* ***

B. Features. Share product/service features (from lined section of item "B" in 4.1a) with respondent and ask the following questions.
1. Which features are most valuable to you (or other customers) and why?

2. What other features would you like to see included?

C. Benefits. Share product/service benefits with respondent (from lined section of item "C" inn 4.1a) and ask the following questions.
1. Which benefits are of greatest value to you (or other customers) and why?

2. Are there other benefits that I have not identified?

D. Marketing. Share marketing methods (from lined section of item "D" in 4.1a) and ask respondent the following questions.

1. Which marketing methods would be most effective in reaching you?
   (How would you [or others] expect to find out about my product or service?)

2. What other marketing methods would you suggest?

E. Pricing. Share price/price range (from item "E" in 4.1a) with respondent and ask the following questions.

If Specific Price:
1. At this *price,* would you/others buy this product?   ___ Yes   ____No
2. If yes, ask, "Would you buy at an even higher price?"   ___ Yes   ___ No
3. If yes, ask, "How much is the most you would be willing to pay?" _____
4. If no, ask, "What would justify my charging this price?" _____

If Price Range
1. With this pricing strategy, would you purchase this product/service?

2. What factors would justify my charging a higher price (or positioning my product higher in the price range)?

G. Quantity.
Ask, "Approximately how many purchases of this product or service would you make in a year?" *Note: Omit this question if purchase would likely be a one-time event.*

G. Demographic information. Ask questions listed on lined section of item "G" in 4.1a and record respondent's answers here.

4.1b

activity
concept testing –
oral survey responses

Directions. Share information included on original survey form with respondent (from "oral survey—interviewer's leads" on previous two pages). Record respondent's answers here

Respondent #3 (name, position, relationship to you.) _____
_____

A. Description. Read product/service description to respondent (from lined section of item "A" if 4.1a) and ask respondent the following questions.
1. Would you purchase this product or service?   ___ Yes___ No

   If **no**, ask, "Why not?"and record response here.
       *** *Even if respondent answered "No" to the question above, have them complete survey.* ***

B. Features. Share product/service features (from lined section of item "B" in 4.1a) with respondent and ask the following questions.
1. Which features are most valuable to you (or other customers) and why?

2. What other features would you like to see included?

C. Benefits. Share product/service benefits with respondent (from lined section of item "C" inn 4.1a) and ask the following questions.
1. Which benefits are of greatest value to you (or other customers) and why?

2. Are there other benefits that I have not identified?

D. Marketing. Share marketing methods (from lined section of item "D" in 4.1a) and ask respondent the following questions.

1. Which marketing methods would be most effective in reaching you?
   (How would you [or others] expect to find out about my product or service?)

2. What other marketing methods would you suggest?

E. Pricing. Share price/price range (from item "E" in 4.1a) with respondent and ask the following questions.

If Specific Price:
1. At this *price,* would you/others buy this product?   ___ Yes   ___No
2. If yes, ask, "Would you buy at an even higher price?"   ___ Yes   ___ No
3. If yes, ask, "How much is the most you would be willing to pay?" _____
4. If no, ask, "What would justify my charging this price?" _____

If Price Range
1. With this pricing strategy, would you purchase this product/service?

2. What factors would justify my charging a higher price (or positioning my product higher in the price range)?

H. Quantity.
Ask, "Approximately how many purchases of this product or service would you make in a year?" *Note: Omit this question if purchase would likely be a one-time event.*

G. Demographic information. Ask questions listed on lined section of item "G" in 4.1a and record respondent's answers here.

4.2 activity concept testing – written survey

A. Develop Written Survey

After preparing and administering an oral survey in activity 4.1, you are now ready to prepare your written survey, which will be administered impersonally (i.e. mail, Internet, handout) to a larger number of people. Test your survey before distributing it by asking several people to complete it and provide feedback on content, clarity, and format. A sample survey is provided in Chapter 14 of textbook.

The following tips will assist you in the preparation of your survey.

- ✓ Use either a cover letter, introductory e-mail, or an introductory statement on the survey document to identify yourself and your reason for requesting respondent's time in completing the survey.
- ✓ Limit your survey to one page (8 ½ x 11 inch, front and back, or 8 ½ x 17, front only).
- ✓ Be sure your written survey document looks professional and is void of any grammatical or spelling errors.
- ✓ Use a reader-friendly professional font; font size should not be less than 10
- ✓ Lead with a clear business concept statement—maximum of 3 sentences; 5 lines.
- ✓ Organize the content categories logically:
  - o What product/service features would be important to them?
  - o What relevant benefits (what will it do for them) would justify a "call to action?"
  - o Why would they buy from you? (demand)?
  - o How would they expect to learn about your business (promotional strategy)?
  - o Where would they expect to find your business (location)? Is that important?
  - o How frequently would they buy/use your product/service?
  - o What price would respondent be willing to pay for your product/service?
- • Create quick and easy-to-use response format within each category of information (checkboxes). If you ask the respondent to rank responses, do not ask that they rank more than 3. Avoid open ended questions.
- • Only ask for relevant demographic or psychographic information.
- • Conclude document with a thank you. Consider including option of them providing contact information, should they be interested in being notified when business is open.
- • Provide a method of easy return to you (i.e. enclosed self-addressed, stamped envelope, e-mail return.)
- • Politely indicate a return date necessary.
- • If needed, make follow-up phone or e-mail reminder requests for respondent to complete and return survey.

Tips contributed by Professor Donna Duffey, Johnson County Community College

B. Administer Written Survey

Survey individuals in your target market (those to whom you plan to sell). Disseminate enough surveys to obtain a minimum of 10 completed responses (more would be better). Provide appropriate lead time. Make follow-up contact to encourage responses as needed.

Note: If you are going to base business decisions on survey responses, you will need to significantly increase the number of surveys administered to obtain meaningful feedback.

C. Compile, Compute, and Report Survey Results

On a blank copy of your written survey form, <u>record and tally survey responses.</u>
Then prepare a written report answering the following questions:
a. How many surveys were sent out/administered? How many surveys were completed?
b. Who was surveyed (describe target market)?
c. What were the key findings of the surveys?
d. What can you conclude, if anything, from your findings? :
e. What changes will you make to your product/service, pricing, marketing, or distribution strategy as a result of this activity?
f. What changes will you make to your survey instrument as a result of this activity?

*Note: Your professor may instruct you to be prepared
to share survey results with class.*

Chapter 15

Business Concept Statement

Developing a Business Concept Statement is an important concluding step to the idea exploration and evaluation process and an important next step in the entrepreneurial strategic planning process. Upon it you will build your Business Plan.

Your Business Concept describes your vision for your business summed up in a few well written, clear, concise paragraphs. As you progress in the planning process, you will share your Business Concept, or its first cousin, the "elevator pitch," with potential customers, vendors, employees, and investors.

Strategic Planning Process

Opportunity Analysis:
Business Ideas – Identification & Evaluation
↓
Business Concept
↓
Business Plan
↓
Launch Business

2/10/2012   Copyright Acheve Consulting Inc.   2

KEY BUSINESS CONCEPT QUESTIONS
Your Business Concept Statement will answer these basic questions:
• What will you sell?
• Who will buy from you (targeted customers)?
• Why will customers buy from you?
• What relevant skills and abilities do you bring to the business?

- How will you market and distribute your products/services?
- When will you be ready to sell your products/services?

Now let's address each of these key questions in more depth.

What Will You Sell?
You clarified this question through the oral and written surveys you just completed in the last chapter. Here you will describe key features and benefits of your business/product.

Features. A product's features include its functionality. For example, your cell phone's features likely include a keyboard, a music player, a camera, a game center, and so on. The list is lengthy. A service's features include the work you will perform for customers. For example, a repair service for cell phones would include the diagnosis of the problem, replacement of parts, and return of the phone through special delivery or at a pick-up counter.

Benefits. Benefits are why customers buy: what the product does for the customer. Key benefits of a cell phone include the ability to stay in touch with family, friends, and the office (phone, e-mail and text messaging), the ability to capture memories (camera and photo album) and entertainment (game center). Key benefits of a cell phone repair service are money savings (not having to purchase a new cell phone), expertise, and convenience (handy location).

Insight or Common Sense
Additional features typically add costs, and higher costs result in higher prices to customers. Make sure the cost of any feature is outweighed by its benefit to customers.

In Pause and Reflect below, describe the features and benefits of your business or product.

Pause and Reflect: Features and Benefits
Identify key features and corresponding benefits of the product/service you will sell in the marketplace.

Who Will Buy From You?

Here you identify your intended target market(s). Remember, from earlier discussions, that small businesses are typically more effective in targeting very specific markets, which they identify through demographic and psychographic segmentation factors. The more clearly you can define and describe your target market(s), the more wisely you can utilize your time and dollars to reach them.

Pause and Reflect: Target Market(s)
Who will buy from you? Identify target market(s) using demographic and psychographic variables.

Why Will Customers Buy From You?

What will set you apart from other similar providers in the marketplace? To distinguish yourself, you need a competitive advantage—something you can provide customers better than others.

Your competitive advantage may rest on a particular business **strength**—higher quality product, better customer service, a convenient location, or more efficient delivery. Make sure you can verify that compared to the competition, you do, indeed, excel in the area you identify. Too often entrepreneurs make such claims without anything to support them. Another me-too business will likely fail.

Your competitive advantage may rest on the **intellectual property** your business creates, which might be a strong brand, patented product, trade secret, or copyrighted materials. See Chapter 2 for more information about intellectual property.

Take a moment to reflect on why customers will buy in Pause and Reflect.

Pause and Reflect: Customer Motivation
Why will customers buy from you?

What Relevant Skills and Abilities Do You Bring to the Business?

Throughout Step 1, you reflected upon previous educational and work experiences, hobbies, and interests to identify aptitudes and abilities you possess. Then in Chapter 11, Evaluating Ideas, Talents and Skills, you assessed personal and entrepreneurial skills and obtained feedback from others on the degree to which you possess these skills. Through this assessment and the screening process that followed in Activity 3.1d, you identified those business ideas which best utilized your talents and skills.

Your choice of a business has been designed to capitalize on your strengths, and it's important that both you and others are clear on how your strengths uniquely qualify you to launch your business. Share this information in this portion of the Business Concept Statement.

How Will You Market and Distribute Your Product/Service?

Marketing describes activities to communicate with your target market(s) about your product/service; distribution describes the actual physical delivery of the product/service. In this part of the Business Concept Statement, you identify planned marketing activities and the business model you will follow to deliver products/services to customers.

Marketing. Following are common methods that businesses use to reach their target market(s) and make sales:

- Advertising: Brochures, flyers, direct mail, newspapers, magazines, television, radio, Internet.
- Promotions: Coupons, rebates, and buying programs.
- Publicity: Press releases to local and regional media outlets, blogs, community involvement, and event sponsorships.
- Sales: Telemarketing, trade shows, sales calls.
- Online marketing: Web site, blog, presence on social media sites.

Since marketing can be very costly in terms of dollars and time, be strategic about the marketing you plan. It all starts with your target markets. How do your potential customers find out about your type of products/services? What do they read? Listen to? Look at? What Web sites do they visit? How do your competitors reach customers?

"In marketing, use a rifle rather than a shotgun to reach customers."

Distribution. The distribution process in some industries is multi-layered, with products passing through many hands on their journey from producer to consumer. These may include wholesalers, distributors, and retailers. For services, the producer typically delivers the service directly to the consumer.

The Internet has drastically changed traditional distribution models in a number of industries, enabling many businesses to sell directly to consumers. Business Web sites, online stores, and auctions facilitate these direct transactions.

Pause and Reflect: Marketing and Distribution
How do you plan to market and distribute your product/service?

When Will You Sell Your Product/Service?

How soon do you anticipant starting your business? Establishing a timeline is critical to projecting your start-up date—when you will be ready to serve customers. To do so, you will need to clearly describe the physical requirements of your business. Will the business be housed in your home? Will you need a retail location? Will you need manufacturing capabilities? What will the physical facility look like?

Even with careful planning, it is likely that it will take longer to get your business up and running than you anticipate. And if a business opens its doors and is not truly ready to meet customers' needs, customers will have a negative first experience, which may end up being their last experience with the business.

Now close your eyes and visualize your business as it will be when you start serving customers and prepare a timeline for arriving at this point.

Pause and Reflect: Physical Requirements and Timeline
Describe your business's physical/facility requirements.

Describe your timeline for starting your business.

Planning is the key to a smooth startup process. Consulting others with similar businesses may enable you to anticipate likely problems. Talking to a "competitor at a distance," a business similar to yours but not in your competitive trade area, can help you uncover hidden challenges and barriers.

PUTTING IT ALL TOGETHER

In the prior Pause and Reflect sections, you clarified key elements of a Business Concept Statement. Now you will put all the pieces together and write a Business Concept Statement for your business. Start by reviewing the sample Concept statement for Scrumptious Pastry Shoppe that follows.

Sample Business Concept Statement
Scrumptious Pastry Shoppe

Scrumptious Pastry Shoppe is an eat-in bakery featuring gourmet coffees and pastries, breads, pies and ready-to-go and special-order cakes. Under the guidance of Joel Garrison, an experienced restaurateur and certified pastry chef, the preparation of gluten and sugar-free pastries provides individuals, families, and businesses, a healthy choice of bakery products. Located in Encino's downtown arts district, customers can either enjoy their pastries and coffee in a friendly, casual eat-in dining area complete with internet access or park in the reserved express pick-up parking spots for quick service on take-out orders.

Opening May 20xx, Scrumptious Pastry Shoppe will be launched with a grand-opening celebration, advertising in local newspapers, flyers and an interactive Web site that displays a broad array of special-order theme options for birthday and wedding cakes and allows customers to place their orders online. Ongoing promotion will include continued local coupon promotions and sponsorship of charitable events.

Student Workbook
Factoring in the information you gathered through your surveys in the previous chapter, complete Activity 4.3, The Key—Business Opportunity that is Right for You, Business Concept Statement.

By preparing your Business Concept Statement, you have the key elements of a well prepared "elevator pitch." With a little polishing, your pitch is ready to share.

YOUR ELEVATOR PITCH

In the entrepreneurial community, you hear the term "Elevator Pitch" frequently. The term is derived from the mythical once-in-a-lifetime opportunity of finding yourself on an elevator with a venture capitalist and having 30 seconds to a minute to dazzle him or her with a brief explanation of your business. Your Elevator Pitch allows you to solidify your business in the mind of the listener and clarify the value proposition you are offering.

Even though you may not be approaching venture capitalists, it's important to have an Elevator Pitch, your business's abbreviated story, to share with everyone from a classmate at a high school reunion to other entrepreneurs at networking events as well as suppliers, service providers, investors, and employees. Your Elevator Pitch can be an effective introduction to share at meetings or your response to "What do you do?" in casual conversations. You will need multiple versions of your Elevator Pitch for it to appear casual and be socially acceptable in the varying venues.

While appearing totally spontaneous, the best elevator pitches are well-crafted and rehearsed. To accomplish this, you'll need to practice and time your pitch, limiting it to thirty seconds to a minute, learning from radio and TV commercials designed to address today's consumers' short attention spans.

Your Business Concept Statement is an excellent starting point for preparing your Elevator Pitch. Follow these tips for preparing your Elevator Pitch:

1. Introduce yourself and establish your credibility. Be brief, yet tout relevant accomplishments.
2. Introduce your business (idea) by providing a high-level overview. This is an introduction to your business (idea), not the time to try to close a sale. Start by identifying the problem or need you are addressing in the marketplace.
3. Gauge interest throughout. Depending on the listener's response, you may share one or two additional facts that validate what you've said.
4. Keep it simple. Your product may employ state-of-the-art technology; but no one cares unless it benefits customers. Speak in terms of benefits, providing technical details only if they are specifically requested.
5. Draw the listener into the conversation. Ask an open-ended question to find out whether or not there is a potential interest. For example, "What about in your firm? How do you handle this?" or "You seem somewhat interested. What else would you like to know?"

6. Assuming some interest on the part of the listener, ask for some type of follow-up. It may be something like, "What are your thoughts about having an initial conversation to talk about this more?" to "How can I get on your calendar?" "May I e-mail you to follow-up on our conversation?"

For more information, see the following Web sites, on which the above information was based:
- "Elevator Pitches: 5 Things You Need To Know," Huffington Post, http://www.huffingtonpost.com/2012/03/15/elevator-pitch-5-things-you-need-to-know_n_1345524.html.
- "How to Write a Better Elevator Pitch," Inc. magazine, http://www.inc.com/geoffrey-james/how-to-write-a-better-elevator-pitch.html.
- Mastering the Elevator Pitch: 5 Tips to Entrepreneur Success," www.IdeaCrossing.org.

4.3

activity

the Key—the business opportunity that is right for you, business concept statement

Directions. Aspiring entrepreneurs need to be prepared to share their business concept with others (i.e. customers, friends, family, colleagues, bankers, service providers, potential investors, and advisors). Answer the following questions in preparation for writing your Business Concept Statement.

	Questions
	What will you sell? (Describe business/product/service.)
	Who will buy from you (targeted customers)?
	Why will customers buy from you? (How is product/business unique? Different?)
	What relevant skills and abilities do you bring to the business?
	How will you market and distribute your products/services?
	When will you be ready to sell your product/service?

Directions. Use the information on the previous page to write a clear, succinct Business Concept Statement, in two to three short paragraphs, to share with others.

Business Concept Statement

Chapter 16

Improving the Odds— More Research

Aspiring entrepreneur Nick Emge demonstrated what it takes to succeed as he conducted research for the restaurant he hoped to open with two business partners. He spent countless hours researching the market—area demographics, industry trends, the competitive environment, and traffic flow and population density patterns in the area. His research helped him decide to continue this entrepreneurial pursuit by writing a business plan and lining up financing.

Now that you have a firm idea for a business in mind, additional research, which you will complete in this chapter, will help you determine if this idea is one you wish to continue pursuing.

ENVIRONMENTAL ANALYSIS

An environmental analysis is an important step in determining the overall timeliness of launching a particular type of business at a specific location. This analysis consists of looking at both the macro-environment, the big picture, and the micro-environment, the small picture, for your business.

The world in which small businesses operate is constantly changing. In Chapter 1, the concept of creative destruction referred to the constant state of change in the marketplace. Compared to larger companies, a small firm's ability to respond to change quickly can be a source of considerable competitive strength. Anticipation and awareness of environmental changes allow small businesses to be proactive instead of reactive.

Macro-Analysis

Macro-environmental changes that are particularly relevant to business include regulatory, industry, technological, social, economic, and demographic changes.

Trade associations can do a great deal to jumpstart your learning curve in these areas.

Through industry journals, newsletters, and conferences, trade associations share this information with their memberships. Earlier in Chapter 13, Activity 3.5, you identified a relevant trade association for your business and were encouraged to contact it to start acquiring information about trends and growth within your industry.

Industry information in the library and on the Internet is often classified by Standard Industrial Classification (SIC) or North American Industry Classification System (NAICS) code. Again, in Activity 3.5, you identified a relevant NAICS or SIC Code that may be useful to you as you begin researching your industry's macro-environment.

Environmental Scan

Macro Environment – National, Global
Economic, regulatory, competitive, technological, demographic, social, industry

Micro Environment – Local, Trade Area
Economic, regulatory, competitive, demographic, business

1/10/2013   Copyright Acheve Consulting Inc   42

Micro-Analysis

This assessment focuses on the environment within the particular trade area in which you plan to operate. You'll want to find out as much as you can about this trade area as it will have a significant impact upon your business's chances of succeeding. Elements of particular interest likely include local regulations, economics, population trends, supply availability, and the competition. Sources for this type of information include

- Census data—state, county, city
- *Survey of Buying Power* (*Sales and Marketing Management* magazine)
- Regional economic reports
- Chambers of commerce

- Local chapters of trade association

Before you invest your time and hard-earned cash in a business venture, invest time and effort in market research.

Student Workbook

Now conduct an analysis of the macro- and micro-environments for your business by completinge Activity 4.4 Environmental Scan.

COMPETITIVE SCAN

The competitive environment within your trade area will have a great deal of impact on the success of your business. To conduct your competitive scan, you will first need to identify a potential location for your business. Then look at the marketplace surrounding that location to identify businesses which offer products that are the same or similar to what you plan to offer. If you plan an Internet, national, or global business, you'll need to broaden your search to identify key competitors in the industry nationally or globally.

Consider both direct and indirect competitors. For example, the direct competitors of a food catering company are other caterers. Indirect competitors are restaurants, hotels, grocery stores that prepare and deliver food, friends and family, and so on. Any of these might make and serve food. Both direct and indirect competitors compete for your business. When an entrepreneur says they have no competition, they usually mean they have no "direct" competition.

You can learn a great deal from your competitors, emulating their strengths and overcoming their weaknesses. All too many entrepreneurs fall into the trap of discounting the competition. Remember, competitors would not still be in business if they were not doing some things right.

Student Workbook

Identify key competitors for your business and a complete Activity 4.5, Competitive Scan.

CUSTOMER IDENTIFICATION

To drill down even further, identify who your first or early customers will be and how you will reach them. In doing so, consider the target market(s) which you described earlier when you wrote your Business Concept Statement in Activity 4.3. Also consider what your challenges will be in attracting early sales. Will you

need to
- Make potential customers aware of your presence in the marketplace?
- Make potential customers aware of their need for your product/or service?
- Attract potential customers away from competitors?

Starting a business with customers ready to buy is the ideal way to begin. Unfortunately, however, entrepreneurs often procrastinate about contacting potential customers out of fear, inexperience, or lack of clarity on who they are or how to reach them. Clearly identifying and reaching out to early customers is critical to successfully launching your business. Within your target market, which customers will you approach first?

Be strategic about selecting your first or early customers by considering factors such as which ones will most likely buy? Be the easiest to reach? Be most receptive to a new vendor? Are influential with other potential buyers?

Your first or early customers can help you establish credibility and, in some cases, open doors for sales to other buyers. Sometimes early customers can act as advocates for your business, providing support and taking pride in your success. Are there customers who are highly respected by others in the industry or community and who would be an asset to launching your business? Spend time thinking about who these customers might be.

Developing a First Customers' Action Plan in Activity 4.6 will help you take steps to reach important early customers. But before developing your own plan, look at the Customer Action Plan that Kathy Yeager prepared to make one of her first sales. Kathy started her consulting business, Contract Training Edge, LLC, to help colleges market and sell workforce development and training solutions to businesses in their communities. You read about Kathy earlier in the Snapshot of Entrepreneur in Chapter 11.

One of the first potential customers Kathy identified was Moraine Valley Community College. She chose this college because it was relatively large, did a lot of work in the area of workforce development, and had the ability to purchase her services. Kathy's Customer Action Plan for this particular client is shown on the next page.

Customer Action Plan		
Potential Customer Name: Moraine Valley Community College		
	Activity to Make Sale	**Completion Date**
1.	Research Moraine Valley Community College on the Web. Identify key decision makers and determine size and scope of their workforce development area, their possible needs, and their territory.	August 1, 20xx
2.	Send an introductory e-mail to decision maker requesting a telephone appointment. Send follow-up e-mails or make phone calls as needed to secure appointment.	August 7, 20xx
3.	Confirm telephone appointment a day before scheduled date.	Day before appointment
4.	Make telephone call. Ask probing questions to uncover client's needs.	During call
5.	Send proposal reiterating client's needs and proposed solutions.	Within 3 days of call

Kathy followed the process she planned and has since conducted one training program for Moraine Valley Community College staff members with another planned in the near future. Kathy maintains contact with this client through regular follow-up telephone calls and through a monthly newsletter she publishes electronically.

Completing Activity 4.6 will help you focus your marketing efforts on customers who can help you effectively launch your business. Identifying the steps you will take to reach targeted customers can help you overcome the inertia and fear experienced by so many new entrepreneurs.

Student Workbook
Carefully evaluate who your early or first customers are likely to be and plan how you will sell to them in Activity 4.6, First Customers Action Plans.

4.4 activity
environmental scan

Directions

It is important to learn as much as you can about your industry and the macro- and micro-environment in which your business will operate. Trade associations, through their journals, newsletters, and conferences, can be a valuable source of this information. Search the Internet or visit the library to locate the names of relevant trade associations and journals. Industry data, classified by SIC or NAIC codes, may also help you answer the following questions.

A. Identify the (type of) business you wish to start. _____

B. Identify relevant industry information.

   a. **Trade association(s).** The following local and/or national trade association(s) is related to my business (idea):

   b. **Professional journal(s).** The following professional journal(s) is (are) related to my business (idea):

   c. **Opportunities.** What opportunities are on the horizon in your industry?

   d. **Challenges.** What challenges is your industry experiencing?

C. Identify relevant factors in the macro-environment.

Identify any national and global factors that may impact your business. Consider regulatory, industry, technological, social, economic, and demographic changes. Include the source and date of information cited. (Note: All may not apply.)

    a. Economic environment

    b. Political and regulatory environment

    c. Industry environment

    d. Technological changes

    e. Social and demographic changes

C. Identify relevant factors in the micro-environment.

Identify micro-environmental changes or factors that are likely to impact starting and operating your business within the trade area in which you will be operating. Include the source and date of information cited. (Note: All may not apply)

    a. Economic environment

    b. Political, regulatory environment

    c. Competitive environment

    d. Industry environment

    e. Customer demographics

4.5

activity
competitive scan

Directions

For your #1 idea, identify businesses that offer the same or similar products or services within your planned trade area. These may be either direct or indirect competitors. An example of direct competition for a greeting card shop is another card shop. Indirect competition includes businesses that offer greeting cards as a sideline, such as grocery stores and gift shops.

For consumer products or services, check your local Yellow Page directory for competitors. For business-to-business sales, you may need to consult a business directory (found in most libraries). If your product or service will be marketed nationally or internationally, use the Internet or library resources to identify competitors.

a. List both direct and indirect competitors below, identifying each business' strengths. (Remember, if a business has its doors open, it is doing some things right.) If the business is a local establishment, a personal visit to the business will be the most effective method of obtaining information.

	Business Name	Location	Products/Services	Strengths
1				
2				

3			
4			
5			

b. How will your business compare to the businesses listed? What is your competitive advantage?

4.6 activity
first customer action plans

Directions. Starting a business with customers in hand is the ideal way to begin. Yet many entrepreneurs procrastinate about contacting customers and beginning the sales process. Having a plan can help you overcome this common tendency. Identify your first customers, focusing on strategically choosing ones who can open doors and help you establish credibility.

	Name	Location	Why Chosen
Customer Identification			
1			
2			
3			

Directions. After reviewing the sample Customer Action Plan in Chapter 16, complete one for each customer identified above, specifying activities planned (i.e. e-mails, phone calls, third-party introductions, direct marketing, advertising, sale calls) and completion dates.

Customer Action Plan	
#1 Potential Customer Name:	
Activities to Make Sale	Completion Date

Customer Action Plan	
#2 Potential Customer Name:	
Activities to Make Sale	Completion Date

Customer Action Plan	
#3 Potential Customer Name:	
Activities to Make Sale	Completion Date

Chapter 17
Next Steps

Before determining where to go from here, first consider how far you have come by reviewing the diagram below.

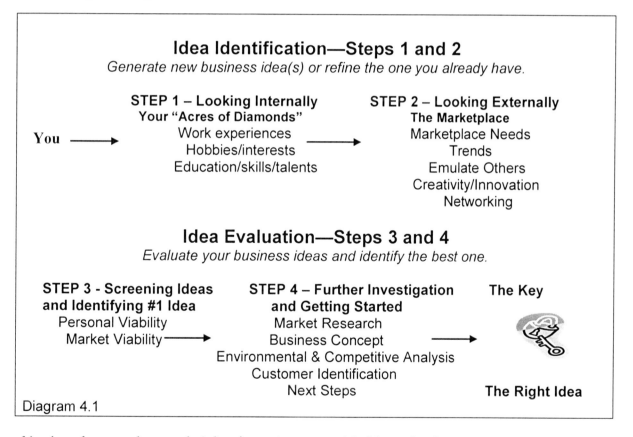

Diagram 4.1

You've done a thorough job of coming up with ideas for businesses by looking at both yourself and the marketplace. You've pared your many ideas down to one or a manageable few. You've examined your strengths and talents and identified which ideas are the best match for you. You've begun your investigation of the marketplace and looked at your financial requirements and funding capabilities. You've gathered marketplace feedback on your planned business. In Chapter 16, you researched the macro- and micro-environments and the competition. The work you have done throughout the book has greatly increased the odds that the business you are considering is the key to your entrepreneurial future.

Now, in this chapter, you'll identify the next steps you will take to move you forward on your entrepreneurial career path.

NETWORKING FOR SUCCESS

Much has been said about networking and its the importance to the successful entrepreneur. Networking opportunities occur continuously, anywhere, and at any time. Effective networkers make an effort to connect with others and to be the first to share or assist, with a goal of creating long term, win-win relationships.

Now is the time to expand your network to include those who can potentially assist and guide you on your entrepreneurial journey. Pay particular attention to meeting and nurturing relationships with people who are knowledgeable about entrepreneurship in general and your type of business in particular.

Most successful entrepreneurs identify one or a series of mentors who have guided them along the way. Consider who can fulfill that role in your life. Such individuals may be other entrepreneurs, professors, or business people such as bankers or suppliers.

Experienced entrepreneurs who offer products similar to those you will be selling may be valuable sources of hands-on information. A "competitor-at-a-distance" may even lead to a mentoring relationship, as happened with one student in an Opportunity Analysis course. His contact with a coffee shop owner over 1000 miles away, who he located through the Internet, resulted in a relationship that spanned several years and helped the student launch his own coffee shop.

Identify a competitor-at-a-distance through the Yellow Pages, Internet, or by talking with others in your industry. In the last case, talking to others may lead to a second-party introduction that can open doors for you and help you become acquainted with others who may be helpful and supportive as you start your business.

Student Workbook
Start networking now by completing Activity 4.7, Networking—Competitor-at-a-Distance.

WHERE DO YOU GO FROM HERE—NEXT STEPS

Working through the activities in this book has moved you toward your goal of starting your own business. But don't stop now. To reach your goal, you'll need to keep going.

You'll conclude this course by reviewing items listed on the sample Start-Up Checklist that follows and then creating your own in Activity 4.8. The value of a checklist is that it keeps certain important items on your radar screen. Assigning a date to each item improves the chances that it will be completed in a timely manner.

Each item on your personal Start-Up Checklist will require careful consideration and, in many cases, the help of experts to assist you in making the best decisions for your business. For items on which you will consult with an attorney, accountant, or other specialist, identify key questions in advance so you can make effective use of your time meeting with them.

Example Start-Up Checklist **Note:** Helpful Web sites are included as a starting point for investigating many of these issues. You can copy the links provided and enter them into your Internet browser. *On many of these items, you will also want to consult an accountant, attorney, or other expert.*	Due Date

1. Choose a business name.
    Helpful Web site:
        www.sba.gov/smallbusinessplanner/start/nameyourbusiness/index.html
	xxx

2. Decide on the legal form for the business (i.e., sole proprietorship, partnership, S Corporation, C Corporation, Limited Liability Company).
    Helpful Web site:
        www.sba.gov/smallbusinessplanner/start/chooseastructure/index.html
    Also see Appendix page 155 for more information and consult an attorney.
	xxx

3. Choose a location.
    Helpful Web sites:
        www.sba.gov/smallbusinessplanner/start/pickalocation/index.html
 	
        www.entrepreneur.com/startingabusiness/startupbasics/location/article73784.html
	xxx

4. Check local, county, state and national requirements—zoning, permits, licensing, registrations. Start with city hall in your area.	xxx

5. Apply for appropriate protections (i.e., copyrights, trademarks, patent). **Helpful Web sites:** www.uspto.gov/ and www.sba.gov/smallbusinessplanner/start/protectyourideas/index.html	xxx
6. Establish professional relationships (i.e., banker, accountant, attorney, insurance agent, other).	xxx
7. Tend to the business aspects of the business (i.e., checking account, business telephone, business cards, stationery, business software, insurances).	xxx
8. Set up your office/location (i.e., purchase equipment, supplies, inventory, signage, fixtures).	xxx
9. Determine if you need a Web site. If so, following are key steps: • Determine your goals for Web site • Decide who will develop it • Register a domain name • Develop the site • Find a Web hosting company	xxx
10. Other:	xxx

A number of helpful checklists on the Internet provide actual links for the information and forms needed. To find them, google "business start-up checklist." For state-specific start-up lists, add your state's name after the word "checklist." Web sites sponsored by government entities or non-profit organizations typically direct you to free resources.

Entire books are written on some of the topics listed on the checklist above. It's easy to feel a little overwhelmed. But help is available from a number of sources, such as the SBA and SBDC, as noted earlier.

"Believe in yourself! Have faith in your abilities!
Without a humble but reasonable confidence in your own powers
you cannot be successful or happy."
Norman Vincent Peale

Student Workbook
Start a next steps checklist for your business by completing Activity 4.8, Start-Up Checklist.

STAYING ON-COURSE

Even with a checklist in hand, many who are interested in starting a business fail to pursue their entrepreneurial goals. Think to yourself, why is this? Write your answer in the Pause and Reflect below.

Pause and Reflect: Barriers
Why do many aspiring entrepreneurs fail to pursue their entrepreneurial goals?

Perhaps you answered time? Money? Feat? Lack of information? Lack of family support? Indeed, all of these can be barriers or challenges.

Speaking to a group of entrepreneurs and entrepreneurship educators, Gary Schoeniger, entrepreneur, speaker, and co-author of *Who Owns The Ice House?* stated that the most common barrier to starting one's own business is "lack of action." He went on to say that "doing nothing, not taking the next step" results in hundreds of thousands of businesses never being launched.

The positive aspect to this barrier is that overcoming it is completely under your control. All you have to do is take the next step, and the next one, and the next one.

> *"The window of opportunity won't open itself."*
> Thomas Fuller

It takes action to open the window of opportunity. There are many reasons individuals fail to take action. One common reason is fear of taking the WRONG action.

A number of years ago, a career counselor, speaking to a group of college educators, compared career success to that of a U. S. space mission. At the time, the United Sates had a very active space program. He stated that on any given space mission, it is estimated that the spacecraft is off course 98% of the time. He said that it is only through a process of "continuous correction" that the spacecraft ever finally reaches its destination. So, too, a successful career requires continuous correction.

The path of an entrepreneur is like that of a spacecraft. You start your entrepreneurial journal with a destination in mind. But only through ongoing marketplace feedback and continuous correction does your business ever succeed.

With each step you take, right or wrong, you learn. **Taking no step is the greatest obstacle to your success.**

This book was designed to help guide you through the early steps of your entrepreneurial journey—one of the most exiting adventures upon which you can embark. Terms such as "the quantum leap" or "taking the plunge" are used to describe the jumping-off point of transitioning from thinking and planning a business to actually starting one. Millions have taken the leap and become entrepreneurs, believing the rewards far outweigh the risks. To see how far you have come, complete the post survey in Activity 4.9 and then compare your responses with those on your pre-survey at the start of the course.

Student Workbook
Complete Activity 4.9, Post Survey. After doing so, go back to Activity 0.1, Pre-Survey, and review your responses to note how your answers may have changed.

As Mark Towers, a guest columnist for *The Kansas City Star*, once commented, "You don't necessarily think yourself into a new way of acting, but rather act yourself into a new way of thinking."

Now is the time that many of you will start acting like entrepreneurs. You have already taken the early steps to do so by completing the activities throughout this book. Success is achieved one step at a time.

> *"When you come to a fork in the road, take it."*
> Yogi Berra

Congratulations!

STEP 4: INTRODUCTION TO FEATURED ENTREPRENEUR—YOU
You are the next featured entrepreneur. How will your story read? Write it on the next page.

Your Story

4.7 activity networking— competitor-at-a-distance

Directions. Through talking with others, searching the Yellow Pages, scanning the Internet, or reading industry publications, identify a business similar to the one you plan to start but outside of your trade area. Contact the owner of the business and conduct an interview via personal visit or telephone.

Competitor-at-a-Distance	
Name of Entrepreneur	
Name of Business	
Address of Business	
Number of Employees:	
Phone #:	E-Mail:
Web site:	Years in Business:
Description of main product(s) or service(s)	

Directions. Choose relevant questions from the list below or develop your own.

a. Who is your target market? How did you identify it? Describe your typical customer.

b. What activities have been most effective in marketing your products/services?

c. Which vendors/suppliers would you recommend?

d. Which trade or professional associations have you joined, and how have they been beneficial to you?

e. What financing sources have been most helpful?

f. How if your product or service priced?

g. How have your products or services changed since you started and why?

h. What were your main challenges in starting and growing the business?

i. Approximately how much money was required to launch your business?

j. If you were to start over today, what would you do differently?

k. May I contact you in the future for additional information?

4.8

activity
start-up checklist

Directions. Identify the next steps you will take to move towards your goal of owning a business. List them here and include a due date for each.

Notice that space is included for only 5 items. This will help you focus on the most immediate/important steps you need to take to move forward. You will want to prepare a more detailed checklist outside of this course.

	Start-Up Checklist	
	Activity	**Due Date**
1		
2		
3		
4		
5		

4.9   activity
post-survey

Directions. Answer the following questions.

1. Do you have an idea for a business about which you are excited and confident?
    Place "x" in the appropriate text box below.

    Yes ☐   No ☐

    If "yes"
    What is your business idea? Briefly describe it here.

    How confident are you that your idea is the right one for you and
    the marketplace? To answer this question, choose a number that
    reflects your level of confidence from the continuum below.

    Write it here. ☐

    Not confident   *Very confident*
        0 ....1..............2.............3..........4........ 5

    If "no"
    What have been the challenges that have kept you from identifying
    an idea for a business?

2. Compare your responses above to those on question 1 in Activity 0.1, Pre-
    Survey. Have your answers changed; and if so, how?

Congratulations on all your hard work
and completing the course!

APPENDIX

- Forms of Business Ownership
- Library References
- Web Resources

FORMS OF BUSINESS OWNERSHIP

Introduction

Even though it is recommended that you seek the advice of an attorney experienced in working with small businesses to determine the legal form of ownership appropriate for your business, an overview of basic aspects of each legal structure will help you use your meeting time with your attorney more effectively. Also visit the SBA Web site for more information at

http://www.sba.gov/content/incorporating-your-business

This Web site also includes links to state forms for registering your business. Another helpful Web site is

www.sba.gov/smallbusinessplanner/start/chooseastructure/index.html

Sole Proprietorship

This is the easiest type of business to form and maintain, requiring no paperwork or approvals. Basically, you are the business, and all profits and losses go to you. There are some restrictions on what can be deducted as business expenses, such as health care premiums, etc., so the attractiveness of this form of ownership is affected by what you want to accomplish with your business. One of the major drawbacks is that you are personally liable for the business debts, which may conflict with your desire to protect your assets. If the business's financial risks or potential liability is significant, consider other legal structures that offer more personal protection.

Partnership

No written document is required, but a partnership agreement is highly recommended, spelling out such things as division of profits, dissolution of the partnership, and outline of duties and responsibilities.

Income and losses pass through to the partners, and they report income and losses on their respective tax returns. In general partnerships, all partners are personally liable for the business debts (all of it, not just your share) AND the actions of other partners.

Corporation and S Corporation

A corporation is a legal entity created by state law. The corporation must operate separately from you and others, and corporate money and records must be maintained separately. Failure to do so can result in corporate members being personally liable.

Requirements vary by state, but some permit one person to fill the roles of stockholder, director, and officer. To form a corporation, a charter must be filed with the state of incorporation.

A corporation may elect to be treated as a partnership for tax purposes (the subchapter S election). In that case, the corporation pays no tax, and the profits pass through to the stockholders and are reported on their respective tax returns. If you make such an election, your corporation is an *S corporation* or a *Subchapter S corporation*. The *S* comes from the subsection of the Internal Revenue Code which permits this election.

Limited Liability Company (LLC)

This type of business entity is designed to combine the benefits of corporate liability protection with the "pass-through" tax treatment and management flexibility of a partnership.

To form an LLC, you must file articles of organization with your state's secretary of state. If no election is made, the LLC is taxed like a corporation.

The advantage of an LLC compared to a partnership is that, generally, the members' liability for the debts of the LLC is limited to the extent of their investment in the business. Since it is a collection of individuals, an LLC suffers from the same limitations on raising capital as partnerships. If structured as such, it can, however, require initial contributions or buy-ins by new members as a way of raising money.

Nonprofit

This doesn't mean that the business does not make a profit. It simply means that the IRS has determined that the business meets the requirement as an organization that provides a service to the community. Purposes include religious, charitable, scientific, testing for public safety, literacy, educational, fostering a national or international amateur sports competition, or the prevention of cruelty to children or animals. In spite of the approval process being long and arduous and requiring the assistance of knowledgeable experts, those starting businesses to give back to their communities may wish to consider this legal structure.

Although nonprofits can pay fair compensation to employees, there are restrictions on distributing net income to officers, directors, and members.

Note: The above information should not be construed as legal advice. Check with a qualified attorney before making decisions regarding which legal form is most appropriate for your business.

Library References

Introduction

The following resources are a sample of what is available at your local library and on the Internet. A reference librarian at the library can assist you in finding these resources. The reference numbers below refer to the Library of Congress system commonly used in college libraries.

Starting a Business

The Business Plan Handbook REF HD62.7.B865. A multi-volume set that includes actual business plans developed by entrepreneurs seeking funding.

Small Business Profiles: A Guide to Today's Top Opportunities for Entrepreneurs REF HD62.7.S621. Covers important information for business start-up, such as costs, expected profits, financing, marketing, and obtaining licenses.

Small Business Sourcebook REF HD2346.U5S66. Lists resources that are important to more than 300 types of small businesses, including start-up information, franchises, trade associations, and trade magazines.

SBA Loans: A Step-By-Step Guide REF HG4027.7.O43. Covers the preparation of SBA loan requests, including loan application forms.

Identifying Customers

Household Spending: Who Spends How Much on What REF HC110.C6 H68

The American Marketplace: Demographics and Spending Patterns REF HA214 .A6

American Generations: Who They Are, How They Live, What They Think REF HC110.C6M545

Demographic and Economic Information

Area chambers of commerce frequently provide information on local growth, traffic patterns, and economic trends.

Rand McNally. Commercial Atlas & Marketing Guide REF G1200.R3. Includes maps, retail sales, business conditions, buying power, transportation routes, etc.

The Sourcebook of ZIP Code Demographics REF HA 203.S66. Reports population counts by ZIP code and provides indexes of spending potential in different consumer categories for each ZIP code.

Statistical Abstract of the United States REF HA202.A5. U.S. industrial, social, political, and economic statistics.

Survey of Buying Power & Survey of Media Markets (Periodical). Annual "special" issue of *Sales & Marketing Management* magazine provides data related to buying power and retail sales.

Local and Regional Companies

D & B Regional Business Directory. Covers specific metropolitan areas, including information on sales, business addresses, number of employees, line of business, etc.

Sorkins' Directory of Business & Government. Covers metropolitan areas, businesses, organizations, and government. Includes company name, executive name, key personnel, kind of business, indication of size by number of employees, and sales range.

Industry Information

Encyclopedia of Trade Associations. Identifies trade associations, contact information, trade publications.

Key Business Ratios, One Year REF HF5681.B2 R25. Offers performance indicators for companies represented by about 800 SIC codes.

North American Industry Classification System 1997 REF HF1041.5.N674. Identifies NAIC codes, which are frequently used to research industry information.

RMA Annual Statement Studies REF HF5681.B2 R6. Covers 300 lines of business, including composite financial statements of companies, presented by SIC code.

Standard Industrial Classification Manual REF HF1042.A55. Identifies SIC codes, which are frequently used to research industry information.

U.S. Industry & Trade Outlook REF HC101.U54. Covers major industries, including historical data and one- and five-year forecasts.

Library Databases/Indexes

ABI/INFORM. Includes reporting and analysis of consumer attitudes, expenditures, marketing, and industry trends.

Business & Company Resource Center. Database for researching topics on business and management. Includes information on consumer behavior and expenditures.

Lexis-Nexis Academic. Includes many full-text business periodicals and reports relevant to advertising/marketing.

Readers Guide to Periodical Literature. Provides indexing and accurate bibliographic data for over 272 popular magazines.

Web Resources

American Consumers (www.newstrategist.com/). Research about consumer demographics and spending patterns.

BizStats (www.bizstats.com). Financial ratios, business statistics and benchmarks, online analysis of businesses and industries.

Bplans (www.bplans.com). Sample business plans and articles on business planning.

Business Owners Toolkit (www.toolkit.cch.com). A how-to for small business.

Entrepreneur magazine (www.entrepreneur.com). How-to guides and information on financial management, business plans, etc. For latest information on "trends," enter "trends" into search box.

Entrepreneurship.org (http://www.entrepreneurship.org). Online international resource designed to help build entrepreneurial economies, sponsored by the Kauffman Foundation. Content and resources for entrepreneurs, business mentors, policy makers, academics and investors.

Inc. magazine (www.inc.com). Information on writing a business plan, starting and running a business, leadership, finance, sales.

Trendwatching.com (www.trendwatching.com. Latest consumer trends United States Department of Labor, Occupational Safety and Health Administration, (www.osha.gov) Information on regulations, enforcement, training, publications and small business. (www.osha.gov/oshstats/sicser.html). Information by industry name or SIC code.

United States Census Bureau

  U.S. Bureau of the Census. (www.census.gov). Comprehensive collection of social, demographic, and economic information.

  American Fact Finders
    (http://factfinder2.census.gov/faces/nav/jsf/pages/index.xhtml). Population, housing, economic, and geographic information.

United States Small Business Administration (www.sba.gov). Starting and growing a small business, loans and grants, contracting, loan assistance.

U. S. Securities and Exchange Commission
  (http://www.sec.gov/info/smallbus.shtml). Information for small business, including forms, regulations, and links.

Urban Institute (www.urban.org). Information on demographic, social, and economic trends.

CPSIA information can be obtained at www.ICGtesting.com
Printed in the USA
LVOW092258090513

332972LV00002B/4/P